BODY BIZARRE
BODY BEAUTIFUL

NAN McNAB

DESIGN BY DAVID ALTHEIM

a Fireside Book
PUBLISHED BY SIMON & SCHUSTER
New York London Toronto Sydney Singapore

for tibby,
who always wants me to wear lipstick.
n.m.

Nan McNab has a great curiosity about the world and writes books on all manner of subjects for children and adults, some fiction, some factual. She has always had a particular fascination for the incredible variety of ways in which people decorate themselves, and why they want to do it.

Acknowledgments

I would like to thank David Altheim first, and most of all, for his generosity and flair in transforming my manuscript into such a stylish book. Thanks, too, to Sue Flockhart for her endless good humor and thoughtful editing, and to Rosalind Price for her encouragement and friendship. Rani Merkel, Bianca Merkel, Emily Flett, Damienne Pradier, Josie Howie, Gwilym Elias, Gina Dimovski, Robin Langer, and Marika Dench shared their stories, their wit, and their humor with me. Andrew Wood, orthodontist; Selby Brown, beautician (Ocean Serenity Beauty Therapy, Anglesea); James Brown, tattoo artist; Rick, tattoo artist; and Sascha, body piercer (Splash of Colour, Ascot Vale); Alan McNab, ophthalmologist; and Jason, body piercer (The Piercing Urge, Prahran) kindly provided professional advice and information. John Nicholson and Tim Oakley made my research a little easier. Thanks also to Nada and Tina, beauticians (Your Body Beautiful, Altona); Fox Body Piercing Studio, Collingwood; Smart Arts, Pascoe Vale; Nikk Crow (OneTribe Body Pierce Studio, Melbourne); Alien Tattoos, Footscray; Karen and staff (Underworld Gym); and performance artist Lucky Rich.

   Last of all I want to thank my little son, Tibby, for his difficult questions, his interest in glamor, beauty, and what is suitable for boys and girls; and my partner, Jiri Tibor Novak, who is indifferent to glamour, but loves beauty.

Cover photographs:

Front cover: A Fulani nomad from Niger checks his makeup in a pocket mirror. He will dance the Yakey, a form of male beauty contest. / A young Australian woman dresses up with jewelry.
Back cover: Fulani women watch men dance at the Geerewol Festival. There, they may select a new partner or husband. (See page 34.)

contents

FIRESIDE
Rockefeller Center
1230 Avenue of the
Americas
New York, NY 10020

First Fireside Edition 2001
Originally published in Australia by
 Allen & Unwin Pty Ltd

FIRESIDE and colophon are registered trademarks
of Simon & Schuster, Inc.

Manufactured in the United States of America

10 9 8 7 6 5 4 3 2 1

Library of Congress Cataloging-in-Publication Data
McNab, Nan
        Body bizarre body beautiful / Nan McNab
        p. cm.
        Includes index
        1. Body Marking. 2. Cosmetics. 3. Hairstyles.
I. Title
GT2343.M44   2000
391.6—dc21   99-059901

ISBN 0-7432-1304-1

Cover and text design by David Altheim
Illustrations by David Altheim

Cover photographs by David Altheim (front right) and
Victor Englebert (front left and back)

BEFORE YOU START

The procedures and activities described in this book could cause harm to your body, and some could be fatal. Don't do anything to your body without first getting help from a licensed professional (and your parents' permission if you are a minor).

The recipes and instructions in the text are meant for information only. Please do not try them at home.

Neither the publisher nor the author shall be liable for any bodily harm that may be caused or sustained as a result of conducting any of the activities in this book.

INtRODUCtION

the BODy QUIZ

Take off all your clothes and stand in front of a mirror.

1. Look at your hair – all of it: head, facial, and body hair.
 A. It is long and natural.
 B. Some of it has been shaved, plucked, waxed, or cut.
 C. Some of it has been colored, permed, dreaded, braided, etc.

2. Now look at your skin.
 A. I've left it as it is.
 B. I've punched one or more holes through it.
 C. I've added some color to it, either temporary or permanent.

3. Fingernail and toenail time.
 A. I cut them when I need to.
 B. They are trimmed, filed, or shaped.
 C. I've added some color, or even fake nails.

4. Smells: Have a sniff under your arms and in any other smelly parts.
 A. I smell as nature intended me to smell.
 B. I'm using deodorant.
 C. I'm using deodorant, or skin cream, or hair products, or perfume, or all of it.

5. Body features.
 A. My body is as it is meant to be.
 B. I wear underclothes that support or shape my body.
 C. An orthodontist or surgeon has altered my teeth, nose, eyes, neck, breasts, etc.

If you have all A's:

You're totally original, or you might be setting a trend. But no major group of people anywhere in the world at any time has left their bodies completely untouched and undecorated. If you have mostly A's, you might be into the natural look, or belong to a religious group, or you might just be lazy.

If you have all B's:

You like to go with the flow, but you don't like going over the top. Or maybe your workplace or school doesn't let you do too much in the way of decoration. If you have mostly B's, you like things in moderation.

If you have mostly C's:

Hey! You're part of a tradition that goes back to the time humans first separated themselves from the apes. And how did they do that? Probably by painting their bodies, cutting their hair, knocking out teeth, piercing or cutting themselves, or coloring their skin. Yes, you've got something in common with most groups of people from most parts of the world.

WHY DO YOU DO IT?

You may do what you do to attract someone. That makes sense – half the world make themselves "beautiful" for the same reason, but nobody can agree about what's beautiful. (Nobody can agree about what's masculine and feminine, either, even though most cultures like the sexes to look different.)

You may change your appearance to show you're part of a group. That's pretty common too, although there are heaps of different groups: male groups, female groups, age groups, sports clubs, style tribes, religious groups, fan clubs, whatever. Or you may just want to say something about yourself – how wild you are, or how weird, or different. Well, people everywhere have changed their appearance to show off or frighten or impress other people.

Then again, you may have done what you did to mark a special time in your life: becoming an adult, falling in love, your greatest achievement, marriage, your first child, grief. Whatever your reason, you've got something in common with almost everybody. Which just goes to show you're a member of the bizarre and beautiful human race.

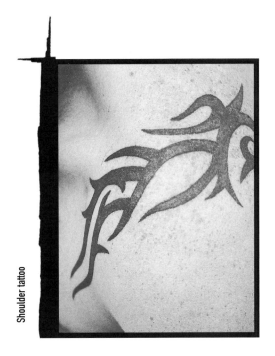
Shoulder tattoo

WHAT'S YOUR LARGEST ORGAN?
WRONG. IT'S YOUR SKIN.

Such a big blank canvas has tempted people to paint, pierce, tattoo, scar, stain, shave, stretch, sew, perfume, oil, and color it for thousands of years. But first you need to prepare the surface.

skin care

Makeup needs smooth, healthy skin as a base. Perhaps you use an exfoliating cream to remove dead skin and freshen up your complexion? Or a pumice stone to smooth those rough elbows and heels? If so, you're continuing a tradition that's over 4,000 years old: In India they used skin rasps made from clay and sand, and there are makeup pots just as old.

Nile Mud Pack
Mix a good quantity of Nile mud with alum and smooth onto the skin. Allow to dry, then wash off with fresh water. Your skin will be smooth and wrinkle free, for a while, anyway. (Alum – aluminum salt – is an astringent that tightens the skin and temporarily reduces wrinkles.)

Ancient Egyptians also washed their faces with a cold cream made from water beaten into wax, oil, and natron, a salt-like mineral.

S K I N

If only they'd had patents in ancient Greece, Doctor Galen would be a rich man. His cold cream is still used as a base for ointments and cleansers nearly 2,000 years after he invented it. Here's the recipe, for free.

Ancient Greek Cold Cream

1 part white wax (beeswax)
3 or 4 parts olive oil
rose petals
water

Crush the rose petals and steep in olive oil. Melt the wax and combine with the oil. Allow to cool, then beat in as much water as the mixture will hold.

Eat me

The Arabs used almond meal instead of soap. In China, women used face masks of tea, oil, and rice flour each night, then powdered their clean skins with rice powder during the day. Roman skin creams contained beans, butter, donkey milk, honey, and wheat. Mmmm.

English rose

The English are famous for fine complexions and a fondness for animals, which might explain why Mrs. Elizabeth Pepys, wife of the famous diarist Samuel, used puppies' urine to lighten her skin.

Beauty and engineering

The Incas dominated Peru before the Spanish conquest 500 years ago. They believed a woman's skin kept its softness if it was washed in the water of her home province. So engineers laid hundreds of miles of pipes and channels from every province to the Convent of the Sun Virgins in Cuzco to bring the girls and young women water from their homes.

Thomas Jeamson offered a cure for red spots in 1665: powdered pigeon dung, flax seed, and French barley in vinegar.

spots and pores

"boys worry about their skin just as much as girls, but they don't come in. they send their mothers in."

selby, beauty therapist

Hormones go haywire in the years between childhood and adulthood, and the result can be breakouts, pimples, acne, blackheads, the works.
A good diet with plenty of fiber and water can help; so can cleaning one's skin correctly, but what to use? Many commercial pimple treatments contain harsh ingredients that are more suited to treating acne than the occasional pimple. They dry the skin, which produces more oil and creates more problems.

"even young people need a gentle cleanser and a moisturizer. some of them think moisturizers are oily, but the right one won't increase their oil levels. they should have their skin properly analyzed, and watch out for 'product push' at some salons. you don't need to spend a fortune, and you don't need a lot of stuff. i like vegetable-based products with no perfume."

selby, beauty therapist

Facials

A deep-cleansing facial helps skin along – it's a booster, rather than a necessity. What's likely to happen to you? You might have a "deep-peeling" cleanse, using a mask and rotating peeling stone to buff off dead skin layers. The same machine has various brush heads for working cleanser into the skin. Another machine opens and cleanses pores with steam. Although it looks like a laser gun from the planet Zircon, it changes oxygen into antibacterial ozone as it passes over an ultraviolet light. For older skin, or problem skin, there are fruit acid peels, and other mysterious-sounding treatments.

And if you already have a bathroom cupboard full of goop that feels like sump oil or makes you break out, don't throw it out – give your legs and feet a treat.

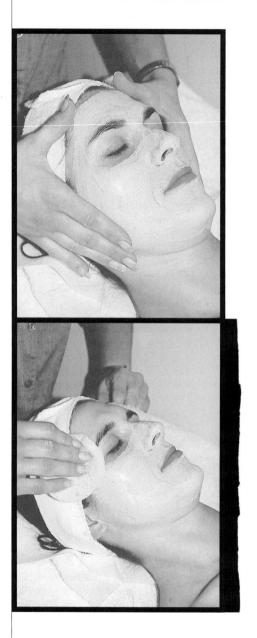

Laughter Lines and Wrinkles

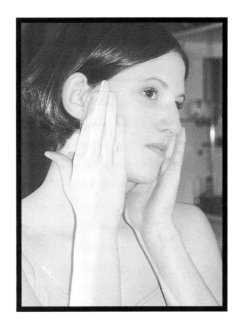

Moisturizers

Once you've cleaned your skin you can moisturize it. Moisturizers leave a film of oil and wax on the surface that helps protect your skin from drying out.

Moisturizers do not stop wrinkles or make them go away. Bad luck. Wrinkles develop in a layer of skin that moisturizers can't touch. Whether you get a lot of wrinkles or not depends on sunlight, your facial expressions (whether you laugh and frown a lot), gravity, and your genetic inheritance. So blame your parents. Collagen and elastin, which occur in the second layer of skin (the dermis), gradually break down, causing wrinkles. So why do people still use face creams? Nobody has ever wanted to grow old, not even the ancient Romans.

Roman women used a lanolin-based night cream to soften their skin – lanolin is the grease from sheep's wool – and Roman husbands complained their beds reeked of sheep. (Today, lanolin is deodorized of all sheepy smells and perfumed.) The Roman poet Horace passed on a recipe for a night cream that doubled as makeup. It included white lead, chalk, rouge, red lead, and crocodile excrement.

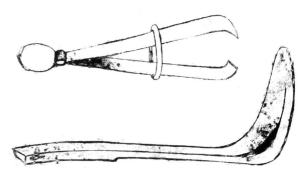

Bronze tweezers and strigil, or scraper, from Roman times

perfume

Archaeologists have dug up ancient perfume pots in Egypt and India and sometimes found a trace of scent after thousands of years. At parties, Egyptian hosts popped a cone of perfumed wax on each person's head. As the night warmed up, the wax melted and released its perfume. In ancient India, both men and women used perfume. Brides were bathed in water perfumed with fruits and herbs, then their bodies were rubbed with perfume and butter – delicious!

The Chinese loved perfumes and even perfumed wine. Top of the perfume charts were lotus, orchid, cinnamon, jasmine, camellia, and other flowers. The Hebrew people used lots of frankincense, myrrh, and other perfumes in religious ceremonies and used a little in daily life – too much and the prophets got upset.

The Assyrians were far more pleasure-loving. They adored perfume, and like the Arabs 1,000 years later, even mixed it into the mortar of their buildings. The ancient Greeks grew or imported many fragrant plants — violets, irises, roses, crocuses, and marjoram — and filled books with perfume recipes. They were not great bathers, and used oils and creams instead of soap.

In the 16th century, European explorers and traders brought back exotic spices and perfumes from newly discovered lands, and the monasteries, which were famous for their herb gardens, produced new and subtle fragrances.

Smells still draw us to some people and drive us away from others. In Papua New Guinea, men and women mix love-magic perfumes with their face and body paints or grease to make themselves extra attractive at courting parties.

Thomas Norton classified 15th-century smells: Roses were cold and good for fevers; violets were neutral; and bad smells from dragons and "men that long dead be" were hot and could cause fever and death.

Aromatherapy

Today, smells are regaining some of their significance in aromatherapy. Many people use fragrant oils in oil burners, bath oils, or massage oils to help themselves sleep, or relieve stress, or feel more cheerful and energetic. There is a fragrance for almost anything you can imagine, and some of them are not so far removed from Thomas Norton's ideas!

Fragrant fingers

The French, Spaniards, Italians, and Portuguese all produced perfumed gloves. Queen Elizabeth I was given a pair embroidered with four roses. The French essayist Montaigne said, "I only need to touch my rather bushy whiskers with my gloves...for the smell to stick for the rest of the day." Catherine de Medici was supposed to have murdered at least two women using poisoned perfumed gloves.

Many women spend a lot of time and money on makeup, but what about men? Is makeup manly? It was once. In ancient Babylon, men (and women) of all ages painted their faces with white lead, used vermilion blusher and eyeliner, and stained their nails and palms with henna. The ancient Persians were equally into makeup, but they used less blusher, or rouge. Persian kings sometimes took their makeup boxes into battle. One Assyrian king, Assurbanipal, wore vermilion on his cheeks, and kohl on his eyes and eyebrows. He plucked out excess facial hair (although in a stone carving of him killing a lion he wears a full, carefully curled beard), enjoyed a dash of perfume, and wore a typically elaborate hairdo.

Even the ancient Egyptians thought a man without makeup was odd. They passed many of their beauty secrets on to the Romans, but not all Romans approved. The poet Ovid scolded men for using makeup or even curling their hair:

"See…that your nails are neat and clean; don't let hair grow out of your nostrils; be sure that your breath is pleasant; and don't go about smelling like a goat. Leave all other cosmetic refinements to women and effeminate dandies."

They didn't listen. Emperors, generals, priests, and ordinary citizens continued to plaster themselves with cosmetics until fairly recently.

face PaiNt

King Assurbanipal

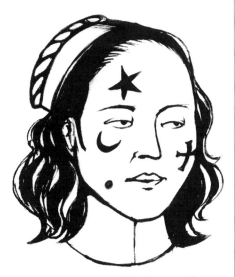

Black beauty patches

A contemporary goth

About 400 years ago, Henri III of France wore thick white makeup and colored his cheeks and lips red; then he dressed his hair with violet powder. Gorgeous.

In 1649 the English puritans killed Charles I, then set about being killjoys for a decade. Makeup, music, dancing, and fun were out. They even introduced a bill into Parliament called "The Vices of Painting and Wearing Black Patches and Immodest Dresses of Women." (Men and women wore small black beauty patches to show up the whiteness of their skin and to cover the odd boil or pimple.)

But men took to wearing makeup again as soon as they could. Even 200 years ago, every gentleman had his box with razors, powder puffs, face lotions, blusher, oil and scent, curling tongs, scissors, and soap.

Nineteenth-century dandies were notorious for their makeup, perfume, and hair oil, as well as their corseted waists and extravagant clothes. But by the 20th century, men's cosmetics had gone underground. Perfume became aftershave, face cream became tanning cream or massage cream, and powder became talc, even if it was skin-colored. Deodorants, shampoos, and conditioners were packaged in rugged masculine colors and given rugged masculine names.

Perhaps goths will reclaim makeup for men, with their decadent pale faces, dark lips, and heavily lined eyes and eyebrows. Cosmetic companies have even created ranges for men who want to be goths.

Cleopatra's cosmetics

Ancient Egyptian cosmetics are very ancient indeed. If you were a wealthy Egyptian, you wore makeup every day. First a foundation of yellow ocher, or orange (for the guys), then eyeliner in black, green or gray, and eyeshadow on upper and lower lids. Different colors for each part were fashionable. Cleopatra blackened her eyebrows and eyelashes and smeared blue-black on her upper lids, green on her lower lids. Eye makeup was supposed to protect the eyes from disease – perhaps it repelled insects, or reduced reflected glare – and the Egyptian word for "eye palette" is linked to the word meaning "to protect." Blusher and lipstick finished off the face, then it was on with the wig and you were ready to start your day. All these cosmetics were perfumed and packed in beautiful cosmetic boxes.

In the Indus Valley, in what is now Pakistan, archaeologists have dug up 5,000-year-old kohl pots and sticks, bronze mirrors, razors, rouge in cockle shells, green eye shadow, and carbonate of lead for skin whitening. There, too, both men and women used makeup. Hippies rediscovered kohl in the 1960s and 1970s, but most people these days use eyeliner instead.

Arabs were supposed to have made kohl out of ingredients such as copper, graphite, lemon peel, coral, pearls, sandalwood, ambergris, bat wings, and chameleon body parts – all of which were burned, then moistened with rose water!

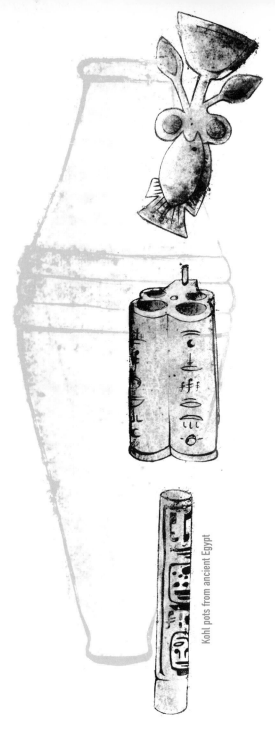

Kohl pots from ancient Egypt

for god's sake

Not all gods frowned on cosmetics. The ancient Hindus offered cosmetics to the Celestial Serpent, and yellow turmeric and a red rorl powder to the gods. They believed makeup colors were magical and life-giving – green symbolized water and plants, yellow the sun, red stood for blood, black for evil passion. Black repelled harmful spirits at funerals and weddings, and was painted on eyes, hands, and feet when people made sacrifices.

Some Hindus believe a third eye exists in the middle of the forehead. A dot of red or yellow pigment called a tilak (or tika in Nepal) is applied at religious ceremonies or at home. It's supposed to bring good fortune, and it may also mean that the wearer leads a pure holy life, or that a woman is married.

But some religions frowned on cosmetics. Some ancient Hebrew texts rejected makeup. It was probably a reaction to their neighbors, the warlike Babylonians and Egyptians, who were really into cosmetics. Here's the prophet Jeremiah reacting to beauty treatments 2,500 years ago:
"Though ... thou rentest thy face with painting, in vain shalt thou make thyself fair; thy lovers will despise thee, they will seek thy life."
    He can't have been very effective. Archaeologists have dug up Hebrew cosmetic dishes from the same period.

Nepali woman

17

Christians were just as critical. They believed "beautification" tempted people to sin. Clement of Alexandria, an early churchman, predicted a bad end for those who were: *"frizzling their hair, anointing their cheeks, painting their eyes and dyeing their hair ... they are not once, but thrice worthy to perish...."*

Christian missionaries took their beliefs around the world, probably stamping out more forms of body decoration and beautification than any other organization. In Australia they tried, unsuccessfully, to stop Aborigines from painting themselves.

Government grouching

A British act of Parliament about artificial beauty is, in theory, still law:

"All women, of whatever age, rank, profession, or degree, whether virgins, maids, or widows, that shall...impose upon, seduce, and betray into marriage any of his majesty's subjects by the scents, paints, cosmetics, washes, artificial teeth, false hair, Spanish wool [rouge], iron stays, hoops, high-heeled shoes, and bolstered hips, shall incur the penalty of the law in force against witchcraft and like misdemeanours and...the marriage, upon conviction, shall stand null and void."

Most British marriages could be annulled on these grounds, although hopefully these modern made-up women wouldn't suffer the punishment for witches, which was often death at the stake!

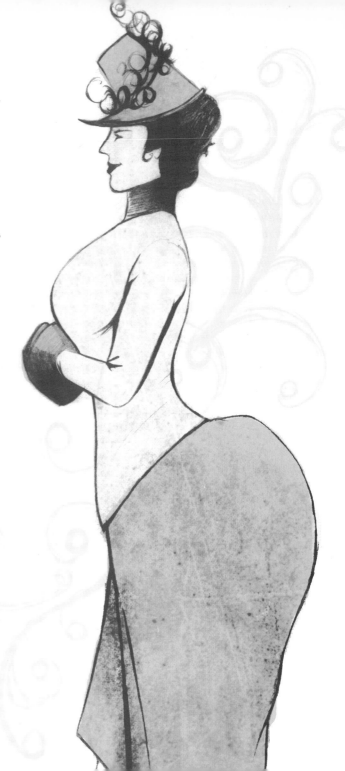

suffering for Beauty

People kept using makeup even when it was packed with poisons – metals such as lead, mercury, and antimony; the poison atropine, from deadly nightshade; and arsenic. Illness, madness, blindness, or even death didn't deter them. The Babylonians' preferred eyeliner was the very poisonous antimony sulfide rather than plain carbon, because it was stickier and contracted the eyelid, making the eye look bigger. In India, women dusted their lips with orange powder made from mercuric sulfide.

Galen, the Greek physician of cold-cream fame, warned people about dangerous cosmetics:
"The excellence of this mercury sublimate is such that the women who often paint themselves with it, though they be very young, presently turn old with withered and wrinkled faces like an ape, and before age comes upon them, they tremble (poor wretches) as if they were sick with the staggers, reeling and full of quick-silver [mercury]."

In the 18th century, the beautiful Lady Coventry insisted on wearing toxic makeup, despite her husband's attempts to stop her:
"At a dinner...he coursed his wife round the table, on suspecting she had stolen on a little red, seized her, [and] scrubbed it off by force with a napkin...." Later, she was seen to have *"laid on a great deal of white which she did not want, and which will soon destroy both her natural complexion and her teeth."*

It did. She was dead by the age of 27, of white-lead poisoning.

Powder puffs

In Asia face powder was made of rice. In 19th-century Europe, you could choose between pearl powder, made from seed pearls dissolved in acid (cheapskates used mother-of-pearl shells), and bismuth powder (a metallic element). Bismuth powder whitened the skin, but sulfur fumes from coal fires turned it black! In 1866 face powder made from zinc oxide appeared – the first cheap, safe powder that didn't discolor.

Makeup today

Some makeup still contains ancient ingredients such as minerals, animal fats, plant extracts, and waxes; others contain modern synthetic compounds, with names like isopropyl lamolate, dehydroactive acid, polyvinyl alcohol, triethanolamine, or imidazolidinyl urea. Don't lick your fingers!

camouflage

Women used to wearing makeup say they feel "naked" without it. So is a naked face more "honest" and individual? Is a made-up face a fashionable mask?

Face paint or makeup can be used to camouflage "weak" features and enhance "good" features. But what is good and bad depends on current trends. Take facial hair: Eyelashes are good (use mascara, dye, eyeliner, false hair); eyebrows can be good or bad depending on the fashion (pluck, wax, or thicken with eyebrow pencil). The ancient Greeks, Etruscans, and Romans liked eyebrows that almost met above the nose. Not for us! Mustaches, beards, and stray hairs are bad for Western women (use bleach or remove the hair), but may be out or in for men. In the 1920s, small mouths were fashionable; now it's wide mouths with fat lips and lots of white teeth.

If you're part of a subculture, the rules are different. Some goths powder their faces white and paint their lips and eyes black, purple, gray, or dark brown to look deathly and macabre. Sometimes they rouge their cheeks heavily to emphasize their corpselike pallor. They may fool around with how males and females are supposed to look, or make themselves up to look evil, macabre, or bizarre. "Making up" is a way of identifying with a group or style, whether you're conforming or out to shock.

on the JOB

For Japanese geishas, beautiful makeup has been part of the job description for centuries. First they apply layers of pink and white paint, then tint the cheeks, eyelids, and the sides of the nose with blusher. Their brows and lashes are dusted with rice powder, and small lips painted in with bright red. A pencil is used to draw in fine sideburns. The eyebrows and eyes are treated first with red and then with black paint, very delicately applied so that only a very little of the red shows. Last, an elaborate black wig is fixed in place. (See color inserts.)

The lips of a geisha

grease paint

Onstage or under studio lights, most men and women wear face paint, whether they're newscasters, clowns, or politicians. Makeup helps movie stars look healthy or ill, old or young, mutilated or mutated, local or alien, human or monstrous. But it hasn't always been so.

In the 17th century, actors used very heavy, crude makeup: bright red on their cheeks and lips, black on their eyebrows and around their eyes, and often blue eyeshadow with white highlights. Greasepaint was invented around the middle of the 18th century, allowing any pigment to be mixed into tallow or hard grease to form theater makeup. Actors use it to create character, age, emotion, and other effects on their faces. (See insert picture of Kathakali actor.)

In southwestern India, actors can take four hours to paint on colorful designs. They use colored powders mixed with coconut oil to turn themselves into gods and demons.

In the famous kabuki theater of Japan, men perform all the roles. Today, instead of masks they wear makeup. Each god, hero, villain, and demon has a particular "face." Women, for example are portrayed using plainer, mainly white makeup. The same goes for the all-male, traditional Chinese opera.

Kathakali actor (See color inserts.)

War paint

Many Native American people painted their faces to look fierce and brave for wars and competitions, and for mourning the dead. They also used it for camouflage on hunting trips. Sioux warriors ringed each war wound with a circle of red paint. The Thompson Indians, also known as Nlaka'pamux, often painted one side of their face red and the other black: The red brought you good luck, and the black brought your opponent bad luck. Only warriors who had killed an enemy had the right to wear black.

paintinc the town red

If it's a party, then pass me the face paint. Swedish children paint their faces to look like witches at Easter. In America, children paint themselves to look like spooks on Halloween. And face paint is often part of kids' parties, festivals, and fairs. Sports fans paint their faces in their team's colors. (See color inserts.) Irish patriots paint shamrocks on their faces and dye their hair green on St. Patrick's Day.

The Huichol people of northwestern Mexico love corn, and festivals. They celebrate planting and harvesting by painting their faces with bright corn-colored patterns representing – you guessed it – cornfields and corn.

Halloween

Imilchil Fair is the highlight of the year for the Berbers of the Sahara, in northern Africa. They trade sheep, goats, and camels and look out for marriage partners. Women and even small girls paint their faces brightly with pink rouge on their cheeks, saffron powder on their eyebrows, kohl on their eyes and noses, beauty spots on their cheeks and chin. (See color inserts.) Berber women don't usually cover their faces, but at the fair they show only their eyes. Men must judge potential partners from the eyes and voice only.

In Mount Hagen, in the highlands of Papua New Guinea, men are the party animals, and the ones who decorate themselves the most. For festivals they paint their faces with charcoal, then add white and touches of red, blue, or yellow around their features. When the women and children paint themselves, they use red face paint and much brighter colors.

For these people, and for other groups, the colors and patterns of the paint relate to other decorations and adornments, such as wigs or headdresses, and are particular to the occasion. Designs have names, and the colors have special meanings. For example, black is often a man's color, and may represent darkness or aggressiveness; red and other bright colors may attract the opposite sex or represent female fertility; white may represent male fertility and attract women.

Andaman Islanders don't settle for simple insect repellents; they decorate their faces with a special insect-repelling paste.

Age of consent
Some Victorian mothers painted their children's faces with white makeup. A century before in France, wealthy children used rouge and makeup as heavily as their mothers. Today, child beauty contestants parade before the judges (and their ambitious parents) in full makeup and elaborate hairstyles.

makeup's makeup

People will use almost anything to change their appearance. Here are some of the ingredients, how they're used, and by whom.

Ingredient	Use	People or place
sperm whale: oil; ambergris secretions	cosmetics and ointments; perfume	West
colored minerals (terre verte, malachite, etc.)	face and body paint and makeup	ancient and modern world
woad (a European herb that contains a blue dye)	blue body dye	ancient Britons
egg whites	hair stiffener	Western punks
honey	skin and hair treatments	ancient Rome, West
henna	skin and hair dye	ancient and modern world
collagen (crude gelatin from bones)	lip-plumping injections	West
talc stone	makeup	modern world
beeswax	hairdressing, cosmetics, hair removal	tribal Africa, ancient and modern world
turmeric	makeup and sunscreen	Middle East
green walnuts	hair dye	ancient Rome

Vain about your veins
The Egyptians, and later the Romans, traced their veins with blue paint to make them stand out. In England, Victorian women used a blue grease pencil, or blue makeup made from chalk, gum arabic, water, and Prussian blue pigment. Rubbing the lines softened the effect.

mouths

"I wear lipstick as a joke. I like dressing up as 'dress-ups'. I wear lipstick like that. I never put it on to make my lips look more red or luscious.... [laughs]"

ROBIN, age 16

None of your lip!

In the West, women are the main lip painters, favoring reds, pinks, oranges, and purples. Occasionally women have their lips tattooed red, perhaps to save time painting them. (See page 45). It's supposed to hurt a lot.

Lip colors come from a whole range of different materials. In India, women chewed betel leaf to redden their lips. Lac, a resin left on trees by the lac insect of southern Asia, was also used as lip color. In the modern world, we use a lot of chemicals and a few tried-and-true ingredients such as tallow, castor oil, and beeswax in our lipsticks, lip glosses, lip pencils, and lip stains.

Black and white

Beauty is never black and white. Some of us have our teeth cleaned, bleached, or capped to whiten them. Elegant Japanese women blackened theirs with iron filings that had been soaked in vinegar for months. The mixture stank, but it blackened the teeth beautifully if it was brushed on every few days. And it distinguished the women from the girls (and the white-fanged animals). The practice was especially popular during the Edo period.

The Naga hill people of northeastern India also blacken their teeth. Long ago in India, women stained their teeth red, and one tribe in Africa, the Fellatah, were supposed to dye their teeth yellow, purple, and blue.

tongues

Tongue paint? Yes – it's part of the face paint used in traditional theater in Calcutta. Some Chinese women reddened the tips of their tongues as part of their daily makeup routine. Maoris liked permanent tongue decorations: They tattooed them — a horribly painful procedure. (See page 43.)

CHINS AND CHEEKS

Forget about chins – everyone else does. And cheeks usually only get a lick of paint. Pink or red seems to be universally popular. Good Christian girls used to pinch their cheeks to redden them. The more daring, or sinful, opted for paint. Even 5,000 years ago people in the Middle East and India would whip out their little cockle shells of rouge and touch up their cheeks. Old-fashioned blushers were made from various red minerals and earths – usually toxic – such as red lead, realgar (arsenic disulfide), and cinnabar (mercuric sulfide). Today, flushed cheeks are less likely to be a sign of poisoning or illness.

eyes

Eyes are supposed to be big and wide-set, at least among most white cultures, and among some black. Certain Asian cultures have always valued small, beautifully shaped eyes. For most people, makeup or face paint helps create the ideal eye.

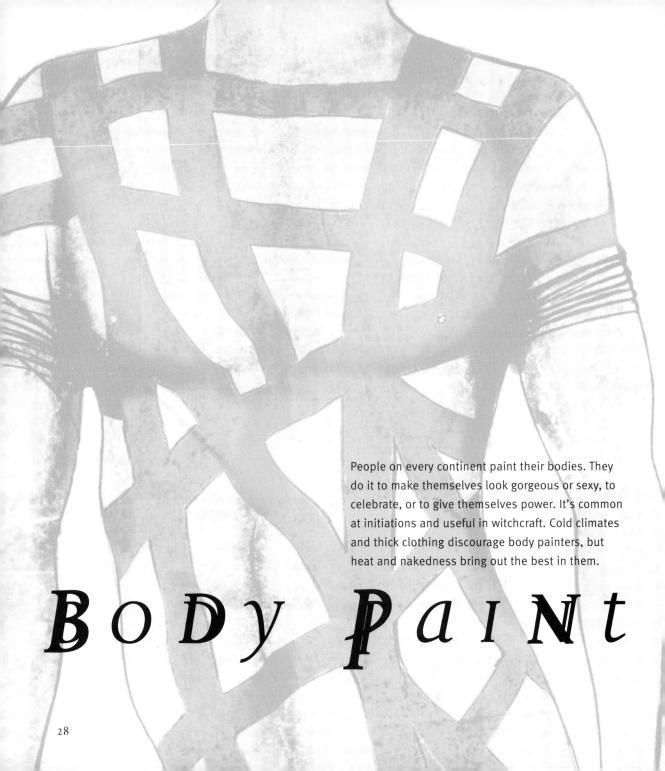

People on every continent paint their bodies. They do it to make themselves look gorgeous or sexy, to celebrate, or to give themselves power. It's common at initiations and useful in witchcraft. Cold climates and thick clothing discourage body painters, but heat and nakedness bring out the best in them.

BODy PAiNt

Body paint may have been one of the first ways we marked ourselves as humans, thousands of years ago. The paint, or ocher, was important enough to carry into the grave. Ancient Saharan wall paintings of people show decorations on their shoulders, breasts, thighs, and calves that were probably paint or scarification patterns. The ancient priests and the learned class in ancient Britain stained themselves blue with woad, a plant dye, and the British may have kept on painting and tattooing themselves until the Normans came in 1066 and put a stop to it. Even body glitter isn't new. Native Americans on Nootka Sound covered their body paint with glittering flakes of mica.

Brown paint
"My skin can look pasty and sick with this blond hair, but the sun's so bad, I'd rather fake it."

Fake tanning products grow in popularity at about the same rate as the hole in the ozone layer. They produce an all-over tan all year round without risking the old UV. And decorative body paint can double as sunscreen or insect repellent.

During the Second World War, when nylon stockings were scarce, many women painted their legs with makeup instead. Some even drew a seam up the back of each leg to complete the effect.

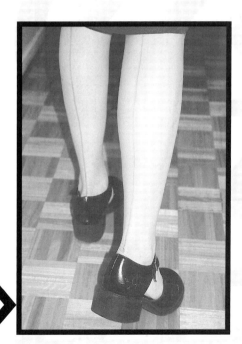

BLOOD AND OCHER

Many of the Aboriginal people of Papua New Guinea and Australia still use body paint made from powdered ochers, charcoal, and clays. (Blood was sometimes used to glue on the finishing touches, such as feathers.) (See color inserts.) Patterns are passed down through clans and contain important symbols from their history and myths.

Painting could start at birth, when some newborns were painted with white clay. Women and men painted their bodies to attract each other, and for rituals and ceremonies such as marriages or initiations. In Arnhem Land, in Australia, body paint still figures in an initiation and circumcision ceremony for boys that takes many days. At first the boys are painted with white ocher, then, as the ceremony progresses, they are carefully painted with their clan designs. On the final day of the public ceremony, their adult guides spray white ocher from their mouths onto the boys' faces. They are then carried to a special secret place to be made men.

Aboriginal boys of the Aurukun people perform the dance of the Beginning of Time.

african art

Among the most skillful face and body painters are the Nuba people of Sudan. Like us, they use face paint to correct flaws in a face or emphasize its good features. For example, if you're a guy with small eyes, you can outline them heavily in black. If your nose is narrow and pointy, you can paint a flattening pattern across the bridge to broaden it. Skillful painters use carefully balanced asymmetrical blocks of color and pattern to create stunning effects.

To celebrate their youth, beauty, and strength, the Nuba people reach for their body paint. The old, ill, or wounded don't paint – they cover up with clothing. There are rules about designs and colors, too. It all depends on your age, clan, status, and state (whether you're pregnant, breast-feeding, married, menopausal). Men especially paint themselves, particularly during puberty and young manhood. Older people are allowed to use more colors, including deep black and yellow; the young keep to simpler patterns and fewer colors.

When people are isolated during childbirth or a particular ritual, such as a funeral or initiation, they do not oil their bodies. Pregnant or nursing women oil and paint only their heads and shoulders. In fact, women rarely paint their faces.

Each clan gathers its own shade of ocher. An inexperienced boy who uses the wrong color usually gets a good thrashing to teach him a lesson. Anyone who persists in using the wrong color risks a crippling disease, or so they say.

The Nuba first bathe, shave off all their body and facial hair, and oil their bodies. Then they apply very beautiful, dramatic designs in colored clays and minerals, using their fingers or brushes of grass or straw. Some of the designs are abstract; some imitate animals or insects. All look fabulous.

photographs:

page 1 top: Novice Buddhist monks at a blessing
ceremony, Thailand

bottom: Jewish men with side curls at the Wailing
Wall, Jerusalem

page 2: Tattoos in the Japanese style

page 3: Yanomami Indian from the Amazon
rain forest, Brazil

page 4 left: Berber woman at the Imilchil Fair,
Morocco

bottom right: Somba *griot* with the facial scarring
that distinguishes him as a member of
his tribe, Benin, West Africa. Griots belong
to a special class of musicians, poets,
and sorcerers.

Essential oil

Oil is such an essential beauty product that when a Nuba girl runs out of it, she stays in her hut until she manages to get some. An unoiled body is a naked body, so an unoiled man wears shorts or a tunic to cover his nakedness. Oil is given as a mark of hospitality, to repay a debt, or as a gift, and it is used for everything from dressing wounds to a health drink.

Touch ups

In the mountains of southwestern Ethiopia, Surma men cover their skin with chalk paste and then draw beautiful, elaborate patterns through the white with their fingers to produce a brown-and-white all-over pattern. Sometimes it's touched up here and there with flashes or lines of ocher. Surma women paint only on their faces and breasts, using white and colored ocher. There are special body decorations for fights or courtship ceremonies, and most of the painting is done after the harvest when the Surma have more leisure time.

Manly beauty

who are the most beautiful men on earth?
"we are," say the fulani of niger.

Each year, when the rains come and the Fulani
have a bit of spare time, they meet for the Geerewol
Festival, a sort of beauty pageant and dating
agency rolled into one. But here it's the guys who
parade and the women who judge. (See the women
on the back cover.)

If you want to get lucky, here's what you have
to do:

First, shave your hairline to enhance your high
forehead, then plait your hair to keep it off
your face.

Make up your face with extreme care: Outline
your eyes and lips with kohl, apply yellow base
makeup, then decorate it carefully with red and
white "flower" designs. Emphasize the length and
beauty of your nose by drawing a fine white line
down the center of it, and you're ready for the
courtship dance.

When you parade before the women, smile
broadly to show your flashing white teeth. If you
can afford gold teeth, so much the better. To
emphasize the whites of your eyes, you may either
roll them or stare wide-eyed at the women.

I'm sure a guy's personality is really important,
too, but if a Fulani woman has an ugly husband,
she may conceive with a more handsome man so
that her child will not be ugly. (Unfortunately, first
marriages are always arranged, so a girl can be
unlucky.) But at Geerewol she can have a brief fling
or meet a second, third, or fourth marriage partner.

**For another Geerewol dance, the Fulani men use red
makeup, paint their lips black, and top it all off with
a fresh white turban and feather.**

Red Indians

Red seems to be a favorite color among the body-painting people of Central and South America. The Yanomami from the Amazon rain forest paint each other in geometrical patterns or motifs from nature. (See color inserts.) These are more than just decoration – they have special meanings. So if you want to send a message to your boyfriend or girlfriend, you can paint it on your body – they're bound to notice.

A lot of red body paint is made from uruci seeds boiled into a paste and rolled into a ball. Men often wear a darker color than women, and both paint their bodies and their hair; even babies are painted. The Karaja from Brazil paint themselves with uruci before visiting their neighbors. Then their hosts paint their faces with uruci and charcoal in welcome.

Many tribes from the Amazon, such as the Shipibo, Achual, and Txukarramae people, paint their faces with red designs. The Moruba paint their faces with black liquid made from charcoal, and wear red or pink face paint in lines under the eyes and across the cheeks.

Very often, colors have special meanings. For the Xingu, red means blood and therefore life, yellow means the sun, and black means night.

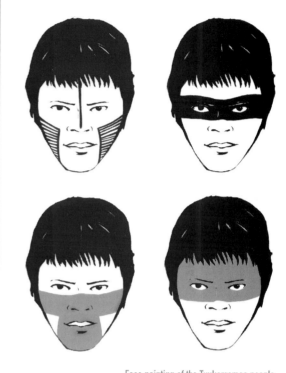

Face painting of the Txukarramae people

During a dry spell, Tenosique boys in Mexico smear themselves with clay and mark rings of ash on their bodies to mimic jaguar fur. Then they perform a jaguar dance, which helps bring rain.

35

asian body art

Almost 1,000 years ago, wealthy Indian women had their bodies and faces painted with colored or black-and-white designs based on plants and animals. Some of the colors were safe, such as yellow saffron (from flower stamens); others were very dangerous.

About 500 years ago, the wallpaper look was all the rage with wealthy Indian women. Complicated designs were cut from fresh leaves and stuck all over a woman's body with oil of aloes. The skin in the gaps was then stenciled with brown and red lac. Poorer people could only afford such costly rituals for important occasions such as weddings.

Indian Sadhus

Most sadhus, or holy men, paint their bodies and faces with tilak, the paint marks of their god. Applying the paint is a ritual that makes the body fit to receive the god's power.

Each sect paints in a particular traditional way, although they are allowed to vary the design slightly. They use ashes or charcoal from a sacred fire, sandalwood, and often dark yellow or orange pigments.

Hindu sadhu, Nepal

finger painting

Rings on her fingers and...tattoos on her hands. People in different parts of the world paint elaborate henna patterns on their hands and feet — sort of semipermanent tattoos. It can take hours. In Bahrain, it's saved for the soles and hands of brides, but in northern India, brides and bridegrooms both use it. Some Indians stain the tops of their feet yellow with saffron and the soles red with lac, then they add toe and ankle rings. Ankles, soles, and hands are decorated in Nepal and other parts of Asia, too. Here's the recipe.

Temporary tattoos

- mendhi powder (available in Indian shops)
- sugar
- boiled water or tea
- lemon juice
- cotton cloth
- oil (optional)

Mix the powder with the water or tea and some of the lemon juice to form a paste. Put the paste into a pastry bag with a fine nozzle. Soak the cloth in a mixture of lemon juice and sugar. Use the nozzle to draw a design directly onto clean skin, as if you were icing a cake. Cover the wet design gently with the wet cloth. When the cloth has dried, remove it, scrape off the paste and, if you like, oil the skin.

If that all sounds too hard, you can copy the early Egyptians, who stained their palms and nails a delicate pink with henna. Or the Assyrians, who used mustard, saffron, and turmeric.

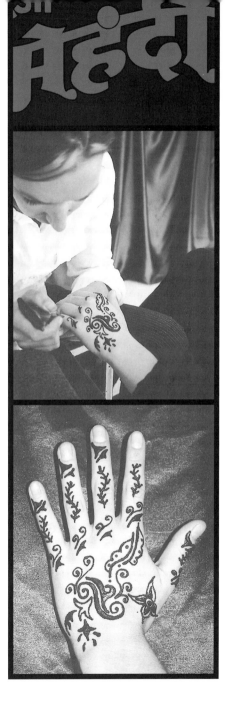

> *"at first i thought it was a mistake...*
> *you know, this is here for Life."*
> *josie, age 24*

Are tattoos permanent? For the first 5,300 years definitely! A man frozen in a glacier in the European Alps over 5,000 years ago still has tattooed lines and crosses on his back, wrist, knee, and ankle.

The oldest tattooing shop, which dated from about the same time, was found in a cave. All the essentials were there: bowls of red and black pigments, sharp flints, and needles made from bone or antler.

Before the frozen iceman was found, one of the oldest tattoos was on an Egyptian mummy named Amunet. She was a priestess to the goddess Hathor at Thebes about 4,000 years ago. When she was unwrapped, she had an abstract pattern of dots and lines tattooed on her belly, thighs, and arms.

A Scythian chief in Pazyryk in Siberia had remarkable and beautiful animals tattooed on his arms, chest, back, and lower legs. They were still there when his body was found 2,500 years later.

Inuit girl

Needlework

The Inuit in Alaska "sewed" tattoos into the skin with a bone needle and a sinew dipped in soot. Even a short tattooed line might require 40 tiny stitches. Youch! An Inuit family, mummified about 500 years ago, had curving lines tattooed on their foreheads, cheeks, and chins. Two, who may have been sisters, had identical tattoos.

tattoos

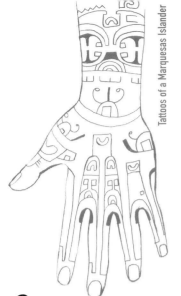

The Tahitians, according to Captain Cook, had a "Z" tattooed on every joint of their toes and fingers, plus circles, crescents, and other designs on their arms and legs. On the Marquesas Islands, a woman could not cook food without tattooed hands.

fierce warriors

The dramatic facial tattoos of the Maori people of New Zealand are called *moko*. Only when a man has proved himself do Maori elders give permission for the tattooing to begin.

In the past, Maori chiefs had their faces and bodies tattooed with elaborate spiral designs to look fierce and impressive in battle. They believed their character was imprinted in their facial tattoos. Tattoos were a sure sign of rank, and could be used as a signature on documents.

Hawaiian warriors were tattooed with spear designs, and the Chinese were tattooing warriors over 2,000 years ago.

Today, tattoos are often worn by groups of would-be warriors: bikers, gangsters, prisoners, skinheads, soldiers, or punks.

In the South Seas tattoos counted for something even after a warrior's death. If you were tattooed, your head was cut off and preserved.

thin - skinned

"It wasn't as painful as I'd thought... Like a little knife cutting in. It stung at first, then it was like a massage with a machine."

Damienne, age 24

Some tattooing methods hurt more than others. Take your pick:

- In Papua New Guinea they rub pigment into cuts
- Pacific islanders tap needles or blades covered in pigment into your flesh
- Modern electric tattooing machines inject ink under your skin at great speed
- Some Japanese use bamboo sticks bristling with needles, whacking your skin twice a second

Certain women in Fiji, Tonga, the Caroline Islands, and New Guinea had their genitals tattooed. According to Captain Cook, Tahitians had their buttocks tattooed black, a painful procedure that was done in one "sitting," but never before puberty.

Samoans endure similar pain during the 18 hours it takes to get their tattooed "shorts." One man said, "For a whole month you are in pain... you walk like a hunchback."

Both men and women are tattooed, and so important are tattoos for traditional Samoans that it is impossible to serve or be apprenticed to a village leader if you are a clean-skin.

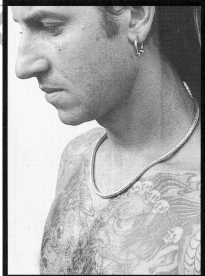

Tattoo gun

The belly button tattoo is still rare. Traditional Samoans regard it as the most painful final flourish to a whole-body tattoo.

SKIN-DEEP

"People do judge you. Lots of men think you're a slut if you have a tattoo. It makes me really angry."

Damienne, age 24

Tattoos have been in and out of fashion. They used to look "rough" and "common." Now, to some people, they're chic. Elaborate tattoos were very popular in Japan during the Edo period, but criminals and prostitutes gave them a bad name. The emperor outlawed them in 1868, and tattooing went underground until the ban was finally dropped in 1945. Today, the trademark of *yakuza* gangsters is a full-body tattoo. Perhaps it began as a reaction against the old practice of tattooing criminals on the forehead with a picture of a dog or some other unpopular animal.

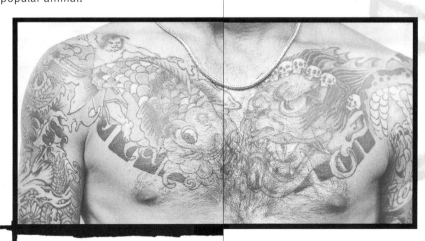

A Japanese-style tattoo

Foreigners were fascinated by the work of Japanese tattooists. Queen Victoria's grandsons, Prince George and Prince Albert, and Nicholas II of Russia went to Japan expressly to be tattooed. They came home sporting dragons on their forearms. (See color inserts.)

41

suffering for art

The word "tattoo" comes from the Tahitian *tatau,* which is derived from *ta,* a mark. In Maori *ta* means "to tattoo, to mark."

"my tattoo's an old chinese character that means perseverance. i really loved the look of it. but first i had to make sure i wasn't putting 'dim sum' on my back."

josie, age 24

Some designs are symbolic: In Japan, carp mean bravery; peonies mean wealth and good fortune. The design is outlined in black, then the colors are filled in. Masters can shade colors by varying the depth of the needles (deeper jabs mean stronger colors). The Japanese preserve about 30 tattooed skins in the medical museum of Tokyo University.

Tattoos may signify an important event, initiation, or rite of passage. Indonesian girls were tattooed as soon as they began to menstruate.

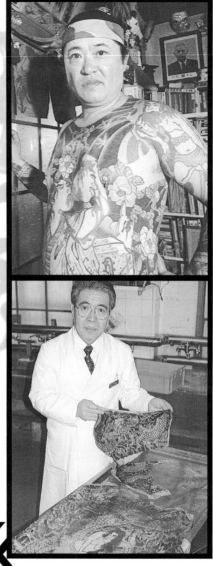

Head of a tattoo club, Japan

Professor with preserved tattooed skin

"It usually means something, even if it's not conscious. Looking back, I'd just moved out of home. I was saying, 'I'm in charge of my life'. It's the only life decision I've ever made."

Josie, age 24

Some royalists had their bald heads tattooed when George V was crowned, and a woman was heavily tattooed with royal portraits, slogans, and coats of arms to honor Queen Victoria's anniversary!

"We got the tattoos on the first anniversary of the death of two friends who died in a car accident. It was a very bad year. We were together when we found out...It took my mind off the day... It was physical pain rather than emotional pain."

Damienne, age 24

When Hawaiians mourned a loved one, they endured the intense pain of a tongue tattoo: lines or a string of diamonds on the rim or down the center of the tongue.

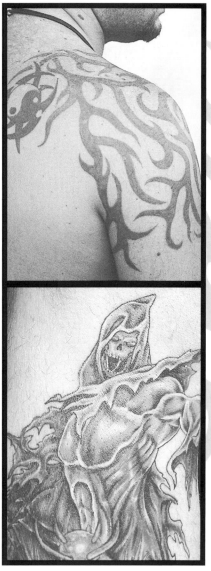

Contemporary tattoo designs

tattoos and authority

"my parents were shocked! my mother totally freaked. she wouldn't talk to me for three weeks, but she's fine now."

damienne, age 24

People in authority have different views about tattoos. Girls and boys used to be tattooed in Europe, but now it's illegal in many countries unless you're over 18.

Christian and Muslim leaders took a stand against it pretty early. People are supposed to be made in God's image, and they didn't want mere mortals adding any graffiti, thank you. Even so, early religious pilgrims often brought back souvenir tattoos from Jerusalem, Mecca, or the Holy Land. One modern religious zealot had the entire Last Supper tattooed across her back, with messages such as "Love One Another" above and below it.

Some Amhara women of Ethiopia still have Christian crosses tattooed on their foreheads and hands. In Hawaii, tattoos could also give spiritual power, or *mana,* and they were an essential part of public life in Samoa.

But in Indonesia, missionaries and the government stamped out tattooing, even though a full-body tattoo used to be essential if you were to make it in the afterlife.

Russian prisoners in tsarist labor camps were tattooed to mark them off from other people, and the Nazis tattooed numbers on many of the people imprisoned in their concentration camps. Slaves that tried to run away from the Romans were tattooed for easy identification. Today, do-it-yourself tattoos are still popular in prisons.

"one girl wanted the backs of her hands done. if she'd had other tattoos, it might have been different, but people would judge her if she was going for a job interview or whatever."

james, professional tattooist

IN YOUR face

Face tattoos have been popular all around the world. Cinta Largas Indians from Brazil have a fine line tattooed below the nose running out to the earlobes.

Mohave Indians wore tattoo marks on their chins, and tattoos were popular in the Pacific Islands. People in Rajasthan believe tattoos protect them from evil spirits.

Arab women may tattoo delicate patterns around their mouths. Maori women tattooed their lips, gums, and chins to avoid looking like dogs with red mouths and white teeth. They also tattooed their foreheads and between their eyes to look younger and more attractive. In the West, women sometimes have tattooed lipstick, eyeliner, or browliner.

In Melanesia, the number of lines in your face tattoo showed the number of your achievements. At one time, if you were one of the Naga hill people of northeastern India, you had to earn a face tattoo by first taking a head in battle.

BE PREPARED

"I WISH PEOPLE WOULD THINK ABOUT WHAT THEY REALLY WANT INSTEAD OF JUST GETTING WHAT THEY CAN AFFORD."

RICK, PROFESSIONAL TATTOOIST

In most parts of the U.S. and Canada, you must be 18 or older to get a tattoo. Tattooists check your age with a valid photo I.D. like a driver's license or passport. Some state or local health authorities regulate and inspect tattoo establishments. Ask your local health department if they do this and only go to licensed shops.

Look for a professional tattooist whose work you like, and take time to decide on a design you'll be happy with. In a good shop the tattoo equipment is sterilized in an autoclave, and new needles are used for each client. The tattooists wear rubber gloves, and the entire shop is clean and businesslike. For more information on choosing a good tattooist, see www.safetattoos.com, the Website for the Alliance of Professional Tattooists.

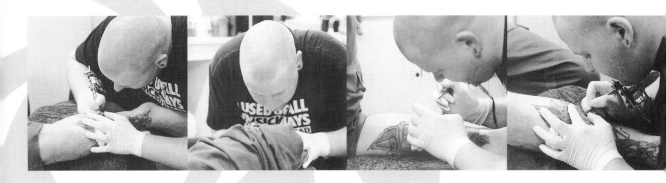

"YOU'RE TRAINED BY A TATTOOIST, AND YOUR TEACHER DECIDES WHEN YOU'RE QUALIFIED. YOU CAN'T TEACH YOURSELF BECAUSE YOU GET BAD HABITS AND YOU DON'T KNOW IT. KIDS SHOULD KEEP AWAY FROM BACKYARDERS...THOSE GUYS GIVE THE INDUSTRY A BAD NAME. I'VE SEEN KIDS THAT ARE SO DISAPPOINTED WITH WHAT THEY GET DONE."

JAMES, PROFESSIONAL TATTOOIST

Several religious groups, including Orthodox Jews and some Christians sects, have strict prohibitions against tattoos and forms of body piercing. Ask about such rules at your place of worship before committing yourself to a tattoo.

Permanent ink

You were young and in love, so you had your lover's name tattooed right over your heart. And now you'd rather forget about it, but you have this permanent reminder....

Injections of urine or mother's milk don't remove tattoos, in case you've heard rumors. Old techniques such as surgery, or rubbing away the skin chemically or mechanically, sound gruesome. Special lasers do remove tattoos, but there's always a small risk of scarring or skin changes. It takes at least half an hour to remove that tiny name, and it's not pleasant without local anesthetic. A tattooist could tattoo something over it – a common solution to problem tattoos – but you've learned your lesson: Tattoos are usually for keeps.

Shoulder tattoos

"BELLY BUTTON RINGS GROW OUT. IT'S QUITE COMMON."

DAMIENNE, AGE 24

If you've run out of places to wear jewelry, you can always pierce yourself. Then you can hang jewels from your ears, eyebrows, nose, cheeks – practically anywhere!

"I'M NOT ALLOWED TO WEAR MY NOSE RING WITH SCHOOL UNIFORM. SOME OF THE OLDER TEACHERS DON'T LIKE IT – THEY TELL ME TO TAKE IT OUT."

RANI, AGE 16

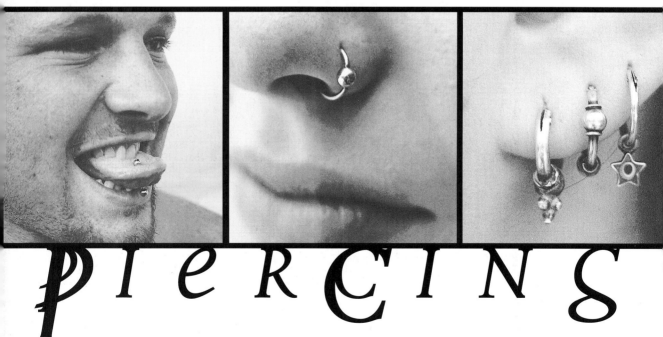

PIERCING

Piercing parallels

Way before the World Wide Web, people all around the world came up with the same bright ideas:
• pierced lips filled with plugs or plates – in Africa, the Arctic, and the Americas
• pierced nasal septums decorated with showy ornaments – in Papua New Guinea and ancient Peru
• pierced ears – on Easter Island statues, in Europe, Africa, South America, North America, Australia – in fact almost everywhere
• pierced nipples – among the ancient Mayas, modern punks, and the English of stuffy Queen Victoria's time.

what's it all mean?

One theory is that people pierce the part they value most. So enormous lip plugs mean the people value eloquent speech; pierced noses mean you value the sense of smell or believe breath is the life force. Who really knows?

Another theory is that evil spirits slip in through ears, mouths, and noses, and the best protection is to pierce the bits that are most at risk and insert protective decorations. Well, they believe it in West Africa. Girls from the Kirdi and Lobi tribes have their lips, noses, and ears pierced in childhood to protect them. Of course, it makes them look more beautiful, too, and you can tell at a glance which tribe they belong to.

A pierced lip symbolizes speech for the Dogon people of Africa. Suya children have their ears pierced so they'll listen to their elders. Then ear disks are inserted to help the child learn. Finally the child's lips are pierced to show that its speech and understanding are improving.

Among the Naga hill people of northeastern India, a jab in the ear and a quick haircut means your dad accepts you as one of the family. Fathers pierce the ears of new babies and cut off a tuft of their hair.

PINS aND NeeDLes

"I've got five piercings in my ears. I did the top one myself — it was really painful."

gina, age 22

These days, special piercing guns fire a sterile metal stud through the skin, more or less painlessly. Do-it-yourselfers try heated needles and corks, with ice blocks to "deaden" the skin first – not always successfully.

You can pierce skin with almost anything sharp, but remember, tetanus and other nasty microorganisms just love puncture wounds, and they can be fatal. Infections can be painful and dangerous and must be treated.

Punks use safety pins to pierce and decorate themselves. In the Amazon pointy sticks are popular. Among some other peoples of South and Central America, it's sharp bones and thorns.

Whatever is used, it needs to be sterile to be safe, and that means more than holding it in a candle flame or dipping it in alcohol. Sterilizing instruments needs to be done by a professional using an autoclave or some other recognized method.

Tired of gold and silver? Some people decorate their piercings with leaves, feathers, or colored wood. Yanomami women and children from the Brazilian Amazon insert fine straws with decorative tips into piercings below their bottom lip. It looks a little like a cat with three whiskers over her chin.

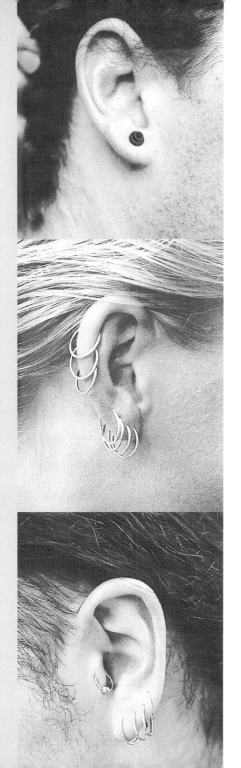

earholes

"I had my ears pierced when I was five. It was my mother's idea, but I agreed. Then I had them done again in elementary school."

ROBIN, age 16

Why do people punch holes in their ears? Pierced and elongated earlobes were a sign of nobility among the Inca. Samburu women in Africa wear double strands of beads looped from their ears for each son who becomes a warrior. Masai women wear earrings to show they're married. Ear piercing can mean many things and nothing at all. It might just be the easiest way to wear earrings.

Men wearing earrings used to be considered completely bizarre, unless they were pirates. Today, many men wear earrings in one or both ears and hardly anyone notices.

Punks have popularized multiple piercings, right around the rim of their ears, and some wear a dozen or so earrings. Today, multiple piercings are commonplace in Western countries, just as they have been in many other parts of the world throughout history.

eLastic ears

Some people want to change the shape of their ears, and one way they do it is to pierce the ear and then slowly stretch the hole. Really huge earrings can leave your earlobes brushing your shoulders.

"It takes a couple of months for those big holes to heal. It's really disgusting. They go pussy, and they smell gross, like damp clothes, only different...."

Gina, age 22

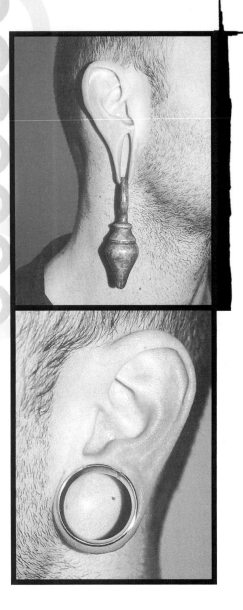

Women from Lamu and Pate Island, in Kenya, stretch their pierced earlobes and wear plugs to keep the holes open. On special occasions they wear gold or silver disks in the holes. In Ethiopia, the Surma pierce and stretch their earlobes: The men wear rings in the gaping holes, and the women force in large plugs 2 inches (5 cm) across. In Borneo, Dayak girls and women pierce their earlobes and stretch them with heavy brass rings. (See color inserts.) If the strain is too much, western Nepalese people wear leather loops over their ears to help support their heavy silver earrings.

The Inca pierced their ears in childhood and began to stretch them with ever larger plugs. But sometimes the earlobe stretched so much it broke. This was clearly a punishment from the gods, and people with torn earlobes were tossed out of cities before important ceremonies, along with the deformed and the dogs!

PICKING YOUR NOSE

"It gets infected because I touch it all the time. I do pick my nose a lot, but it's just playing with the stud. It's very fine, and it lies flat against the nostril."

gina, age 22

If you pick your nose as the perfect place for a piercing, you're not alone. Nose piercing has a long history. Nose studs have been dug up from Indus Valley civilizations of 4,500 years ago. In Africa gold nose ornaments from 1,200 years ago have been found, similar to those worn today in West Africa. The Maya people of Central America pierced their nostrils, earlobes, and lower lips and hung wires, animal teeth, beads, chains, and rings from them.

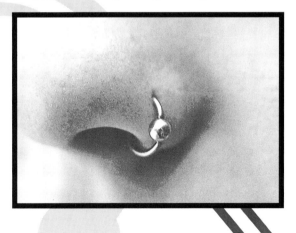

"I had my nose done this year. It was a present from my friends. They blind-folded me...then walked me into the place and there's this guy with tattoos all over him...he put a needle in first, then pushed the stud in. He had something up my nose, then he pushed till he bent it. It was really painful. I went green, and my eyes rolled back...."

gina, age 22

Nose piercing may be significant, or decorative. It may identify a group, such as the Native Americans from the Pacific Northwest called the Nez Perce (Pierced Nose) tribe, who wore shells in their noses. In Africa, elders of the Turkana and Pokot tribes wear aluminum leaf pendants in their noses to announce a daughter's engagement. (See color inserts.) In India and Pakistan, women may wear beautiful filigree nose ornaments through their pierced nostrils or decorated gold or silver rings. This jewelry may indicate a woman is married and wealthy. Sometimes fine chains link nose jewels to earrings or hair decorations.

In the Brazilian Amazon, children and adults of the Maruba tribe pierce their nasal septums and thread them with strands of fine beads. The ends loop across their cheeks and behind their ears, a bit like droopy whiskers. In some New Guinea tribes, older men have their nasal septum pierced so they can wear shells, pigs' tusks, feathers, or bones, each of which may be both a decoration and a symbol. Some Australian Aborigines also pierced their septums. Indians near Nootka Sound pierced their nasal septums and wore lengths of soft cord through the hole. They also pinched the septum with thin horseshoe-shaped decorations of iron, copper, or brass that hung down on their upper lips. One group even managed to wear big plugs through holes in the top of their nostrils!

In the early 1980s punks pierced their noses to be defiant and nonconformist, and a stud in the nasal septum is still sort of "in your face."

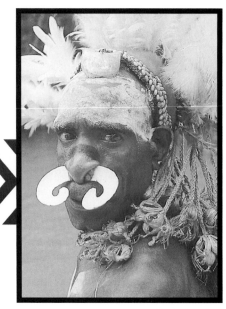

Warrior, Irian Jaya

Cuna Indian girl, Colombia

54

BRISTLING BROWS

"If you pierce between your eyebrows it can make your face numb. It can be very dangerous."

saseka, BODY PIERCER

Eyebrows, like most other parts of the body where you can pinch up a fold of skin, can be pierced. They were popular only with punks, but now lots of people are wearing rings or studs through their eyebrows. But beware! Eyebrow piercings should be done only on the outer third of the brow. If the piercer makes a mistake, the facial nerves running under the brow near the nose can be damaged, leaving your face permanently numb.

"I went with a friend, to a place in the hills. It was like an adventure. We went out on the train. I thought it'd hurt much more. I felt really faint, saw dots, you know, but then I came to. When I walked out the wind pulled at the eyebrow ring, but it was cool. It felt pretty good. Pretty cool. At home I walked in and mom and dad said, 'Son, what have you done to yourself?'"

gwilym, age 17

Danger Zones

Some health departments check piercing equipment and procedures, but in many areas piercers aren't required to pass inspections or hold licenses.

Piercers train as apprentices to experienced piercers, many of whom are also tattoo artists. Check with your local health department for their regulations and be sure to go to a reputable piercer.

Infections and irritations are the most common problems from piercings. They generally result from poor aftercare, such as overcleaning, undercleaning, or using the wrong antiseptics.

An inexperienced piercer can go too shallow, and the piercing can grow out in a week; or he can go too deep and damage tissue or nerves. For example, women's nipple piercings should not go through the areola, or milk ducts can be blocked and cause breast-feeding problems. And incompetent genital or nipple piercings can reduce sensitivity.

"you have to be careful of veins in the cartilage at the top of the ear, and you need to feel the skin carefully before using the needle so that you don't pierce where you will do damage."

sascha, body piercer

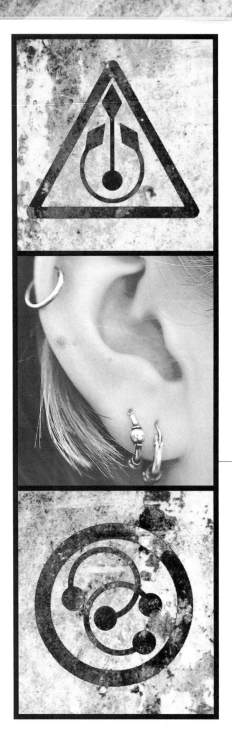

In most places professional piercers will work only on people 18 and over, though this isn't a legal requirement. Piercers try to avoid problems with unhappy kids and their angry parents by dealing only with legal adults. But some piercers will accept younger clients who have written permission from parents or who have a parent present at the piercing – and they check carefully to make sure it's a parent and not a friend.

"parents will generally find out about a piercing because it may be a little bit tender. It's best to get their consent. parents are good at helping kids look after their piercing properly."

JASON, BODY PIERCER

"Kids should think it out really carefully first and come in with their parents' and school's permission. We get them phoning up on Mondays saying, 'The school says I have to take it out! What can I do?' The answer is nothing. They have to take it out. But if it's looked after properly and they get one they really enjoy, that's great."

Jason, body piercer

Piercers have to be careful about needle-stick injuries – they use needles rather than a piercing gun – and everything must be thoroughly sterilized to prevent HIV, hepatitis, and other infections.

Body piercings are generally not as robust as ear piercings. They can't tolerate too much swapping around of jewelry, and the jewelry should be a good fit and not snag on clothes. Tongue piercings swell, so a long barbell should be used first, then swapped for a short one.

button your Lip

"my friend had his bottom Lip done. they clamped his Lip, pierced it, then put the barbell through and screwed the ball on the outside. it's flat on the inside."

gwilym, age 17

Studs and rings through the bottom lip are a popular item today, but would you go so far as a lip plug?

Young Surma women of Ethiopia have their bottom lips pierced when they are 20 or so. It hurts, and they risk infection. A small disk is inserted, forcing the lip out and down, in the start of a spectacular pout. This is replaced over the course of a year with increasingly larger disks, sometimes reaching 6 inches (15 cm) or more in diameter and pulling down the woman's cheeks and top lip. (See color inserts.) Women talking together may remove their plates, but not when there are men around. (Their lips look like saggy elastic.)

No one knows the origin of this custom, but the size of the plate is connected to the number of cattle asked for the bride price. The women see it as a way of bringing wealth to their parents: Really big plates are worth up to 50 cattle. But if a young woman becomes pregnant before her wedding, she is forbidden to wear a lip plate, and her lover is forced to marry her and pay her parents with cattle.

The shape of the plates has changed over the years from wedges or trapezoids to circles, but the custom is otherwise unchanged. Other tribes have given up lip plates or the women have replaced the huge disks with small plugs. One story has it that the lip plates were to deter slave traders, but there is no evidence either way.

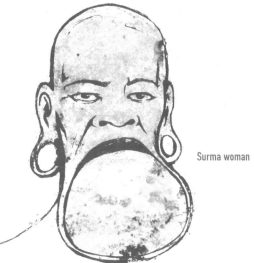

Surma woman

A lot on his plate

In the Brazilian Amazon, it's the men who wear lip plates. Txukarramae Indians are eventually able to insert wooden disks up to 5 inches (12 cm) in diameter into the holes in their lips. Unlike the Surma women, they tilt their disk up so that it juts out toward their nose, making clear speech difficult (and kissing pretty much impossible). The disks are made of lightweight wood called sara. (There's a coincidence – the Sara people of Chad also wear lip disks.)

Karamojong men in Uganda wear a different style of lip plug – the lower lip is not distorted, but supports a large aluminum ornament that sits in front of the chin – a bit like screwing a huge decoration onto a modern lip-piercing bolt.

The Shipibo Indians of the Brazilian Amazon wear silver lip ornaments through their lower lips, and Eskimos wore plugs either above or below their lips.

Anuak women of Ethiopia wear more modest lip ornaments – a thread of beads hangs from their pierced lower lip and mingles with the array of beads they wear around their necks.

BeLLy ButtOns

"my BeLLy Button was a reaLLy Big issue. a DOctOR friend did it at home with an anesthetic. i know, it's a Bit wussy. he used a special tapered needle.... [whatever is inserted] can grow out – it's quite common. the Body pushes it out if it gets infected."

damienne, age 24

Belly button rings and studs are very popular now. Gluing jewels in may be okay for belly dancers, but a ring is more permanent.

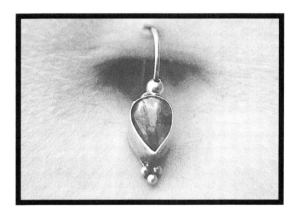

"the navel stud is in an awkward position for healing since it is covered with clothing and stays moist. i put a curved Barette through the skin above the BeLLy Button because there is less friction than a ring."

sascha, Body piercer

tongue tied

Tongue piercing? Okay, poke out your tongue and we'll clamp it. Hold still. Now, this can be quite uncomfortable. It will be swollen for three or four days and takes about two weeks to heal.

Remember, in that time there should be no exchange of body fluids, and that includes kissing.

"when people come to me and their tongues are green and pussy, i tell them to stop kissing their girlfriend or boyfriend...."

sascha, body piercer

Maya people pierced their tongues regularly to get blood for ceremonies and rituals. To increase the blood flow, they would draw a string back and forth through the hole.

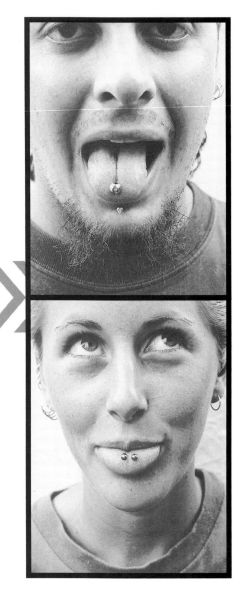

Nipples and Genitals

"I've had one nipple pierced and it isn't half as sensitive as the other."

michael, age 17

Piercings through the nipples or genitals can seem appealing, but they can also reduce the sensitivity of these parts.

The Dayak men of Borneo had their penises pierced at puberty and things inserted into the foreskin. After sitting in a cold river for a long time, the penis was clamped between two slats, each with a hole drilled through it, and then pierced with a sharp bamboo spike. The boys' grandfathers then inserted a *palang*, a stud with a lump at each end, through the hole in the glans, and the boy was eventually decorated with a tattoo, which meant he wore a *palang*.

English men during Victorian times would have their penises pierced so they could anchor them to the leg of their tight trousers, so as not to spoil the line.

Young Roman men, especially homosexuals, decorated their nipples with gold! They'd learned it from those beauty experts the Egyptians.

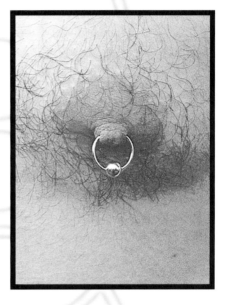

In the 1880s, worried parents wrote to the *Family Doctor*, an English magazine, complaining that boys were having their "breasts pierced and rings inserted in them, at a foreign private school." Apparently the boys were also having their ears and noses pierced and decorated. By 1899, *Society* reported on the latest craze for men and women — breast piercing. Who said the Victorians were stuffy?

Today, men and women have their nipples pierced and wear rings, studs, or other decorations through the holes. In some cultures, this is a traditional form of decoration; in the West, it's a fairly new trend.

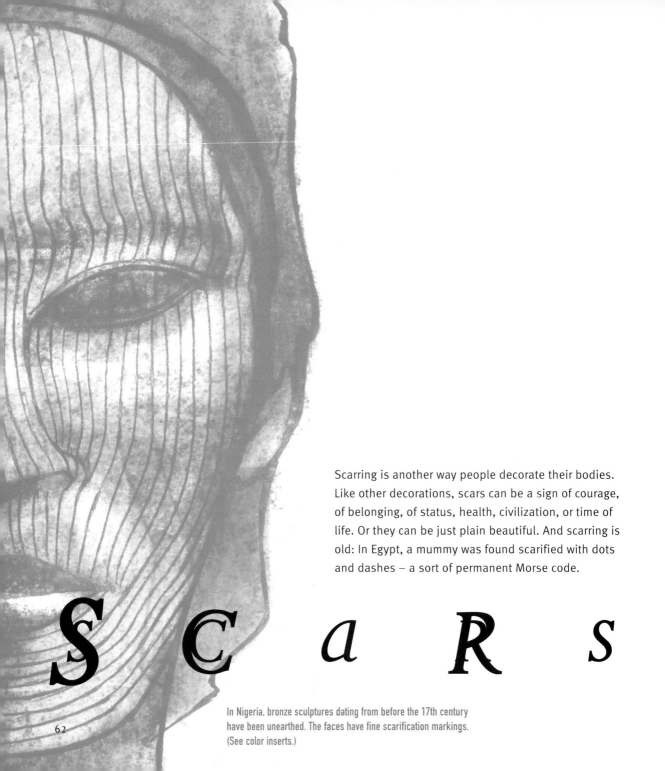

Scarring is another way people decorate their bodies. Like other decorations, scars can be a sign of courage, of belonging, of status, health, civilization, or time of life. Or they can be just plain beautiful. And scarring is old: In Egypt, a mummy was found scarified with dots and dashes – a sort of permanent Morse code.

SCARS

In Nigeria, bronze sculptures dating from before the 17th century have been unearthed. The faces have fine scarification markings. (See color inserts.)

Hooked?

Some girls can't wait to get breasts; others wish they'd never appeared. But in Sudan, Nuba girls have another reason to study their chests. As soon as the bumps appear, the girl is carted off for some permanent skin treatment.

The scarifier takes a sharp thorn, hooks it into the girl's skin, pulls it up, then slices it off. (And you thought injections hurt!) The more the skin is hooked up, the better the scar will be — nicely raised and long-lasting. Rubbing ashes into the wounds helps too. Eventually a pattern of dots covers the girl's breasts and belly, right down to her navel.

Then she begins to menstruate, and she's off to the scarifier again. This time it's the whole front of her torso.

Having a body that feels like bubble pack is pretty desirable, and the young woman is soon married and pregnant. After her first child is weaned, and she's ready for sex again, she really gets the works: scars across her back and buttocks, the backs of her arms and neck, and her thighs. Even at one scar a second, this last set can take two long days. She may faint from pain and loss of blood, but you won't hear a squeak from her. Until she gets the bill! A full set of scars is very expensive, but they're worth it. They make her so desirable that she's more likely to be whisked away by a lover now than at any other stage of her life.

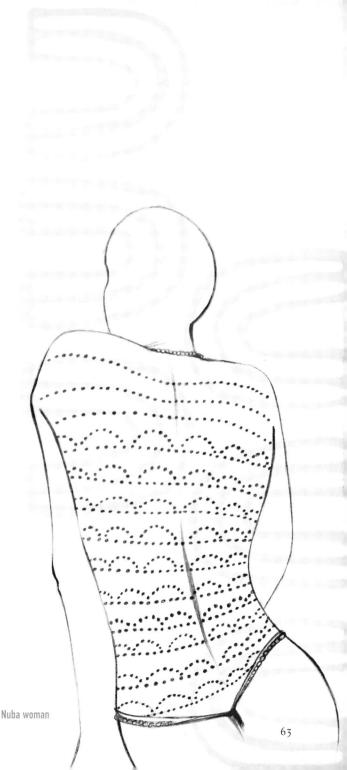

Nuba woman

63

Scarification was once all the rage in Africa. But some governments have now banned it, and young people moving to the cities are giving it up, along with their tribal ways. One day, all bodies may feel more or less the same.

A good set of scars appealed to Australian Aborigines, too. Sharp stones, shells, hot stones, or coals would do to make the wound. You could choose between the flat look or the raised look by treating the cuts in a particular way. Fighting, mourning, and decorative wounds could all be treated with ashes, clay, or grease to emphasize them. And then people could read you like a book: The scars told them your group, your special skills, or your status. For example, boys were often scarified as part of their initiation, then again as they learned more of the law.

Both men and women scarred their torsos and upper arms with regular lines and patterns. Sometimes people even slid pebbles or other bits and pieces into the wounds.

Dueling scars

Until the last century, German university students — the boys, not the girls — had a reckless way of scarring themselves. They slashed at each other with dueling sabers, and if they were really lucky, they got a good long gash on their faces. This was seen as terribly manly, and they would pour wine into the wound to exaggerate the scars.

BRANDING

Will it catch on as body decoration? Ask the cows. The Persian emperor Darius, who lived 2,500 years ago, branded cuneiform letters on the brows of 4,000 Greek prisoners. Before the Emperor Constantine, the Romans branded slaves, criminals, and deserters on the forehead. Then Constantine explained that humans were made in God's image and should not be defaced, so slaves were branded on the hand or leg (must have been a great relief).

The French were keen on branding criminals, too. Crooks sported a fleur-de-lys on the shoulder. By the 18th century a thief (voleur) was branded with a V, convicts sent to the galleys were branded with GAL, and a beggar (mendiant) was branded with an M.

English, French, Dutch, Spanish, and Portuguese slave traders all branded slaves with their master's initials each time the slaves changed hands.

Branding is still fairly rare. Some groups use it as an initiation rite, and there are do-it-yourselfers who just want to try something different, but results can be disappointingly blurry, and it hurts.

INSERTIONS

Nervous about your jewelry being stolen? Try wearing it underneath your skin. Some people have a bracelet inserted under the skin of their wrist, or have a series of bumps inserted in a line across their skull under the scalp. The ancient Maya of Central America were keen on insertions – they used to slide pieces of bone, rings, or colored stone into the glans of a man's penis. Groups that practice scarification often used inserts to enhance the size and beauty of the scars. The Burmese wore magic amulets under their skin, and some groups have worn jewelry under the skin of their chests.

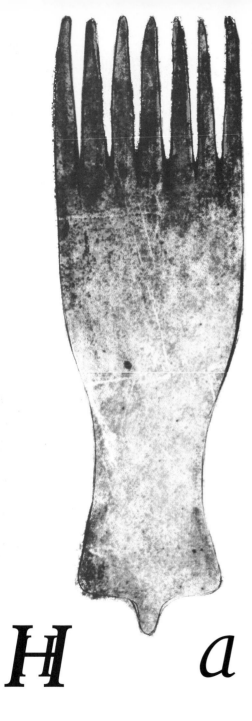

People have always fiddled about with their hair. Old combs – 4,500 years old – have been dug up from Indus Valley civilizations. Noblemen in ancient Sumeria wore gold dust sprinkled in their hair. The ancient Egyptians used curling irons, hair dye, and wigs. The Assyrians knew just as much about hairdressing and recognized the craft 5,000 years ago, perhaps because they were mad about fancy hairstyles. They perfumed their hair with oregano, and dyed gray hair with cassia seed and leeks. Over the centuries and around the world, hairdressers have come up with an almost endless variety of hairstyles, and often the hairstyles tell us a lot about the people wearing them.

H a I R

Style tribes

In Africa, you can sometimes identify a person's cultural group by his or her hairstyle:

• In Angola, Mwila women wear their hair in hundreds of braids around their head. Some put butter on their hair to keep it glossy, then dye it with red powdered bark.

• The Mangbetu women of central Africa traditionally arrange thin braids over a light, cylinder-shaped metal frame and decorate it with long needles made of bone. It takes hours to finish and is left untouched for weeks.

• Masai warriors in Kenya wear their hair in hundreds of long, twisted strands smeared with fat, red ocher, and clay. They can spend 15 to 20 hours styling each other's hair.

• Wealthy Senegalese women lengthen their hair with sisal fibers and dress it with butter and crushed charcoal.

• In West Africa, cornrowing (braiding the hair close to the scalp) and threading (wrapping sections of hair with thread) are popular. Westerners like them too. Apparently the practices are over 4,000 years old.

• The Surma people of southwestern Ethiopia crop their hair very short, then shave strips from the ears across the hairline at the front and back, or shave all the head, leaving only a patch on the crown or a strip from ear to ear. Shaved heads are a mark of beauty for both sexes and any age. The Nigerian Igbo people cut geometric patterns in their hair, a little like rappers.

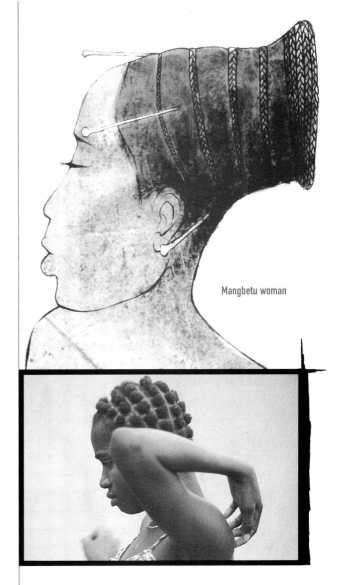

Mangbetu woman

• The Hamar people of southern Ethiopia make elaborate hairstyles called *boro* to celebrate a successful hunt or crop planting. The hair is trimmed and colored with clay, then colored powders are flicked on with a brush.

• The Turkana men of Africa twist their hair into small plaits with clay and shape it into buns on top of the head. Ostrich feathers are woven in as a sign of status.

• In Namibia, Himba boys and girls wear their hair in braids along the sides of their faces. When the boys have enough experience and independence, they wear one braid on each side of the head. Married women weave lengths of their brothers' hair into their braids.

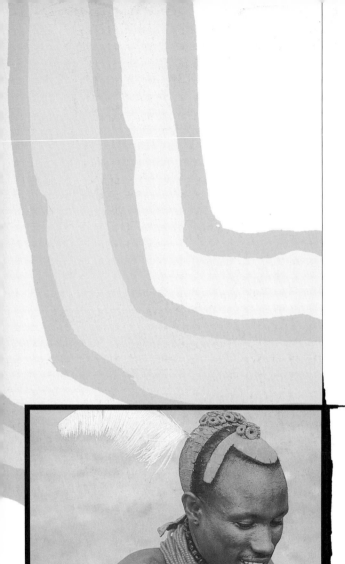

Turkana nomad, Kenya

Across the globe in South and Central America, some tribal groups cut their hair in a circular shape and coat it in red urucum paste. Some people, like the Txukarramae, grow their hair long but shave their heads above the forehead. Indian women in the Andean regions of Bolivia, Ecuador, and Peru often wear thick plaits and bowler hats.

In Europe, hairstyles were often regional. German girls from the Black Forest traditionally wore their hair pulled back smoothly from their face, tightly plaited, then wound round the head.

In Brittany, some women still take half an hour or so to wrap their hair in velvet and insert it into a traditional tall lace cone, called a coif, on top of their heads. Hairstyles had a lot to do with class and wealth, too. Wealthy European women's hair was often styled into soaring shapes over hidden frames and decorated with bizarre items such as live butterflies in cages or clockwork toys.

Even today, different groups wear different hairstyles to show they belong: Rockers slick back their hair; hippies let it hang long and "natural" or henna it; skinheads shave their heads; punks go for Mohawks and bright colors; and rappers like razored patterns and styles.

French hairstyle, 1776

A punk with a Mohawk

Bad Hair Days

Ever think your hair's a curse? You're not alone. The Nuba of Sudan believe enemies can use their hair for sorcery, so they carefully bury all their body and facial hair clippings. They also believe that witchcraft can make your hair fall out.

Western witches were said to gain power over a person if they had a lock of their hair or some nail clippings.

Rapunzel
Tzotzil women in Mexico save their hair combings in a bag so that they can climb to heaven on a rope of their own hair.

The Inca king Pachacuti had a servant to collect any of his fallen hair and eat it, because it was too sacred to lie about on the ground.

Even after death hair is important. Nuba corpses have their hair dressed to prepare them for the afterlife. In Papua New Guinea, ancestors are supposed to live in people's hair: If it grows well, your ancestors like you; if it doesn't, you know who to blame. In Queen Victoria's time, the English wove the hair of the dead into elaborate shapes and made it into things like flower arrangements or brooches, and wore locks of it in lockets.

A 19th-century brooch containing a lock of hair from a loved one.

Power hairdressing

Hair is often linked to power: Men show their body hair and look powerful; women remove their body hair and look childlike and powerless.

• In the Bible, strongman Samson lost his power when Delilah cut his hair.

• In New Guinea, wigs are supposed to give power and attract women. Wig making is kept secret, and the wig maker is not allowed to have sex while he is working on a wig. The wigs can be complicated constructions of human hair caked with clay, fringed with animal furs, greased and brightly painted. (See color inserts.)

• Aztec warriors of Mexico wore only a ridge of hair on their heads to show they'd taken many prisoners.

• Sumo wrestlers, the strongest men in Japan, wear a special topknot, which many believe gives them extra power. When they retire, their hair is ceremonially snipped off.

• Most modern soldiers have very short hair, perhaps to remove their individuality, or to show their obedience, or just because it's easy to take care of and out of the way.

Zulu warrior, 1910

Short-haired soldier

Sumo wrestlers

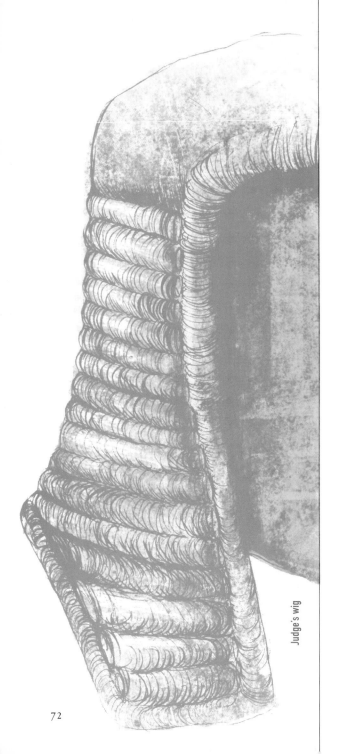

Judge's wig

• Young Samburu warriors in Kenya wear braided, mud-plastered hair to indicate their status and role as warriors. (See color inserts.) Men are divided into age groups: Every seven years, if they are worthy, they move to the next group and change their hairstyles.

• French kings used to wear their hair long in the belief that it gave them power.

• Many Celtic warriors of western Europe wore their hair long — it was a mark of honor. When the Romans conquered them, Julius Caesar ordered haircuts all around.

• Doctors, judges, lawyers, and military officers once wore different kinds of wigs to show their profession and their rank.

Hair is also linked to fortune. Nigerian children with thick, curly hair are supposed to bring good luck. Turkana women from Africa sew wooden pendants into their hair for luck. Some Indians offer a lock of their hair to the gods for favors, and lovers have always offered locks of their hair to each other. Strange that toenails have never had the same appeal.

Fur, feathers, and fingernails

Fingernails, fur, feathers, hair, and hoofs are all made of the same stuff — the protein keratin — in case you've forgotten your links to the animal kingdom.

the godhead's hair

Why do so many religions make rules about hair? Shave it! Cover it! Don't cut it! Hair goes hand in hand with vanity, individuality, sexuality, and other bodily things, whereas religions usually emphasize humility, modesty, and spirituality.

Many Orthodox Jewish babies have their first haircut at three years of age, sometimes at a festival called *Lag b'Omer*. Hasidic Jewish men do not shave and wear earlocks, or side curls, hanging in front of their ears, following the Torah's rule against cutting "the corners of one's beard." (See color inserts.) Many married Orthodox Jewish women keep their hair covered, either with a *sheitel* (wig) or a *tichl* (kerchief). This symbolizes their faithfulness to their husbands.

Muslim women cover their hair and sometimes their faces; Buddhist monks and nuns shave their heads, and so do some Christians. (See color inserts.) Hindu holy men don't cut their hair, and neither do Sikh men – they cover it with a turban. Amish men do not wear mustaches, and some never trim their beards.

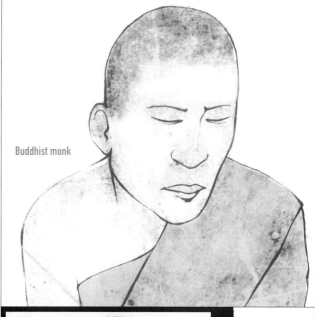

Buddhist monk

The turban-veil of Muslim Tuareg nomads of the central Sahara acts as protection against sandstorms. The blue dye comes off on their skin, also protecting it from the sun.

DREADS

"I'D WANTED DREADS FOR SO LONG. THEY ENDED UP COSTING $300! IT DIDN'T WORK THE FIRST TIME. MY HAIR ENDED UP IN RINGLETS, SORT OF FLUFFY LOOKING, LIKE SHIRLEY TEMPLE AND FUZZY BEAR. THEN THEY DREADED BY THEMSELVES."

EMILY, AGE 16

Rastafarians wear dreadlocks, but not all dreadlocks are worn by Rastafarians. Rastafarians also consider marijuana a holy plant, which has given dreadlocks a bad name. In the British Virgin Islands, foreigners with dreadlocks are expelled, and in Zimbabwe a dreadlocked lawyer was barred from court for two years because of his hair.

"YOU GRAB A CHUNK OF HAIR, TEASE IT REALLY VICIOUSLY, THEN WRAP IT GENTLY ROUND A PIPECLEANER TO HOLD IT TIGHT. YOU NEED TO GET THE ROOTS REDONE AFTER ABOUT SIX MONTHS — THEY GROW OUT STRAIGHT. THAT HURTS. YOU HAVE A SORE SKULL AT THE END."

"WITH DREADS COMES DANDRUFF. WHEN YOUR HAIR GETS WET, YOU CAN'T DRY IT. PROBABLY MY HAIR IS, LIKE, MOLDY."

"I HAD IT DONE IN THE HOLIDAYS. THEN I'M LATE FOR CLASS AND EVERYONE TURNS AND GOES 'OH MY GOD!' AND THE TEACHER GOES 'WOW! THAT'S FANTASTIC!' I FELT LIKE A NEW PERSON."

EMILY, AGE 16

A girl with dreadlocks

turning a hair

"I did it with a friend at home. first blond, then green. it faded after a week or two. i'll dye it again...for a change. change is fun."

gwilym, age 17

Change your hair, change your life? It often works in reverse. Sometimes new hairstyles marked important changes for whole societies. In 1912 Chinese politicians outlawed the long "pigtails" or "queues" men wore because they symbolized the ways of the old rulers.

Weddings change lives, too. Traditionally Chinese brides had their hairline plucked the day before their wedding, then wound the long braid they'd worn as single women into a bun at the nape of the neck. Until this century, young European women also "put up their hair" when they married. In Japan, single and married women wore different hairstyles, too. A Hindu groom covers his bride's hair-parting with red powder to indicate that she is married. In Cambodia a little hair is cut from brides and grooms at wedding ceremonies. Then it is perfumed and passed through a gold band to remove evil. Among the Hopi Indians, the groom's godfather is symbolically scalped at the wedding. Afterward, the bride changes her squash-blossom whorls (two big curls of hair like a butterfly), which she'd worn to show she was marriageable. At traditional Korean weddings, the groom used to wear a transparent woven hat of his father's ancestors' hair. With each death more hair was added to the hat.

And in Africa, hairstyles can indicate not only a woman's marriage status, but also how many children she has. Rendille women in the northern desert of Kenya wear their hair in a crest shape caked with mud, animal fat, and ocher to show they've given birth to their first son. When their son is circumcised to indicate his maturity, the woman shaves her head.

To mark perhaps the biggest change of all – death – in Papua New Guinea, Mount Hagen men who have lost a son wear their hair messy and unwashed as a sign of mourning. And in Angola, women mourn by wearing strings of beads wrapped around their hair like a turban. In China, women in mourning sometimes wear white flowers in their hair.

Hopi Indian girl

reBeLLIOUS HaIR

The people of Madagascar used to cut their hair when their king died, but in the 1800s a group decided they didn't want a new king and refused to cut their hair. They were called the Tsimihety — those who don't cut their hair.

In the 1920s, "modern" women began to cut their hair short to symbolize their increasing freedom and power.

During the 1960s and 1970s people, in the United States especially, began to wear frizzy "Afro" hairstyles to reject white ideals of beauty and protest against the treatment of blacks. About the same time, hippies and other kids wore their hair long to protest against war. In 1967 the Greek government banned long-haired tourists from entering Greece to protect the local people from their "bad influence." In the 1970s British working-class kids protested against the establishment by wearing elaborate, brightly colored punk haircuts.

Men have short hair and women have long hair, right? Wrong.

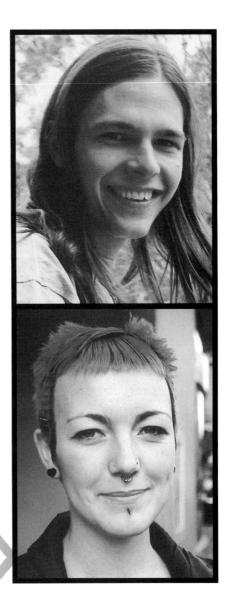

Baldness —
Don't Laugh!

The Roman Emperor Domitian was a vain man. He wrote a manual on hair care, but soon afterward he went bald. He crucified anyone he caught making jokes about his hairlessness, or slowly burned them to death. Domitian was not a popular man; his wife helped murder him, just before his forty-fourth birthday. Other Romans were more laid back about their baldness. Some painted hair on their heads or bought a wig.

Men have always worried about baldness, and "cures" keep springing up, many of them involving food – curry, cheese, avocados, fat, garlic, cows' livers, and chickpeas – usually rubbed on, not eaten. In the 17th century, men tried a mixture of bees and wasps burned black and mixed with oil (perhaps it looked like hair when it was painted on). They've also tried crocodile or snake fat, vinegar, dogs' paws, hair-transplant surgery, toupees, and hairpieces. Here is a baldness cure popular in 17th-century Europe.

Baldness is genetic: Testosterone (the male hormone) acts on the scalp of some men and switches off their hair follicles. Only masculine men go bald! And yet men still continue to spend billions of dollars each year on treatments. Hair transplants are one of the commonest forms of plastic surgery for men. But the Brotherhood of Bald Men in France is determined to enjoy baldness – members celebrate it with bald beauty contests.

Baldness cure

2 oz (60g) bear grease	2 oz oil of scorpions
2 oz hedgehog grease	2 oz badger grease
1/2 pint (285ml) olive oil	

Combine all ingredients and apply to the scalp.

WIGS AND WIG MAKING

Romans loved wigs of blond German hair, and there was probably plenty of it after Julius Caesar's wars pushed the boundary of the Roman Empire up to the Rhine River. He had his enemies' heads shaved to show his mastery. Among the Germans, shaving was a punishment for adultery, so it would have been doubly humiliating. It was a windfall for the wig makers of Rome, though.

Caesar's lover, the Egyptian Queen Cleopatra, also wore a wig. Wealthy Egyptians shaved their heads and wore stylized wigs colored dark red, blue, or green. The most ancient wig is about 5,000 years old, found in an Egyptian tomb.

The Christian Church, predictably, was opposed to wigs: Clement of Alexandria claimed that blessings stuck in the wig and didn't get through to the person underneath! Despite this, people continued to enjoy wearing wigs, none more so than Elizabeth I of England, who died in 1603. She had about 80 different colored wigs, and had her own hair dyed red for good measure. For the next 200 years, European men, women, and even children wore wigs. Hair became so pricey that children and young girls were snatched, shorn, and their hair stolen. Wigs were often huge, and powdered white or gray, although this became less popular in France after the French Revolution in 1789. Powder was linked to royalty, and royalists lost more than their hair at the guillotine.

Wigs didn't begin to look natural until after the 18th century. By then, hair collectors were cutting poor peasants' hair and selling it to wig makers.

One Hindu temple in India makes nearly two million dollars a year selling hair that is cut off pilgrims by a team of barbers working all day and night. The pilgrims offer their hair to the Hindu god Lord Venkateswara, but it ends up in wigs for mere mortals.

Not all wigs end up on heads. Smooth-bodied male disco dancers wear chest wigs to fill the gap in their open-necked shirts. And pubic wigs, or merkins, were popular in Europe in the 17th century and again during the Second World War among prostitutes.

Egyptian wig

False hair

"when I was mad I spent $600 on getting waist-length plaits. I get bored and want to change my appearance. If I'm honest, I like to be outrageous and try different things. they were really heavy, but they looked really african and exotic. easy to care for. my own hair started falling out of the plaits — they cut them, then unwove them."

damienne, age 24

Today they're called extensions, but 400 or 500 years ago, European men and women were adding false "real" hair, or yellow or white silk, to their own hair to thicken it. Young Hmong women weave black wool, cotton, and hemp into their own long hair, then wind it around huge combs shaped like sacred buffalo horns.

PHOTOGRAPHS

page 1 top left: Aboriginal boy from Injinoo (Bamaga, Cape York) applying ceremonial body paint for the Laura Dance Festival, Australia

bottom left: Samburu warrior with earplugs, scarification, and the braided hair of a young warrior, Kenya

right: Mud-men warriors from the Solomon Islands, South Pacific

page 2 left: Turkana elder with aluminum leaf pendant, Kenya

top right: Padaung woman with neck rings, Thailand

middle right: Dayak girl with earlobes stretched by brass earrings, Central Borneo, Indonesia

bottom right: Surma woman with large lip disk, Ethiopia

page 3 top left: Boy painted and dressed as the Hindu god Hanuman – the sacred monkey god, India

bottom left: Rugby fan painted in his team's colors, Australia

right: New Guinea wigman of the Huli clan, Southern Highlands, Papua New Guinea, with cassowary feathers at the top of his wig

page 4 left: Performer from the Kathakali dance theater in full costume, India

top right: Geisha with makeup, kimono, wig, and hair ornaments, Japan

bottom right: Devil mask for the carnival procession on the Day of the Dead, Peru

Color

"when you dye your hair it's so much fun. I like having different colored hair."

rani, age 16

Even if you keep all your hair, you will probably still go gray, and not everyone enjoys it. One popular Roman hair dye used very fresh green walnut skins and juice. (Check out the color of pickled walnuts and you'll see why.) If they wanted to bleach their hair, they used alkali from strong soaps and sat out in the sun for hours on end.

Indians dyed their hair with Indian madder, a plant that produced red dye. Dogs' urine, kept in a glass for four or five days, was supposed to dye the hair a darker color.

Dinka men in southern Sudan bleach their hair yellow with ash and cow urine. Near the Hunza River in Kashmir, men use henna to dye their hair and oil from apricot kernels to brighten it.

"at the moment it looks dull. usually I've got at least one color in, so I'm slacking off. in the old days I'd dye the top of the dreads red and the bottom purple. I used to put tinsel in, and wraparounds in different colors."

emily, age 16

Deadly dye

If you're dying to dye your hair, check out the dye carefully — it could be fatal. Some hair dyes contain lead acetate, which may give you cancer. Hair dyeing must always have been a risky business. Two thousand years ago, Ovid wrote smugly to his mistress: "Didn't I tell you, 'Cease to dye your hair'? And now you have no hair to dye."

Marie-Antoinette, who lost her head to the guillotine in 1793, wore orange powder in her hair, which, by lamplight, made the hair look red. At the time, there were recipes published for several different colored hair powders: brown, blue, violet, pink, and yellow.

BODY HAIR

"I've never shaved — always waxed, say every six weeks. It doesn't hurt anymore. Your bikini line hurts. I do it myself once or twice a year in summer. You get ingrown hairs...and it's disgusting. I've been doing it so long I don't question it."

Josie, age 24

Waxing and waning

Girls may visit a beauty salon first for a wax treatment – their legs, eyebrows, or "bikini line." And the guys? Where men visit beauty salons — and it's often only in big cities that they do — waxing can be the most common treatment. Wives and girlfriends ask them to have their chests and backs waxed, at least that's the men's excuse.

"I love waxing cyclists — their legs are so nice and taut."

Selby, beauty therapist

Cyclists aren't the only sportsmen who go in for waxing; bodybuilders often have all their body hair removed to emphasize their muscles and veins. Some women remove underarm, leg, and pubic hair, as well as facial hair, because their culture frowns on female body hair.

If you can't face wax, there's always the razor. Razors are probably the oldest method of removing hair, and stone knives were probably the first razors. Copper and later bronze razors were dug up from the Indus Valley civilization of 4,500 years ago.

In ancient Rome, both men and women removed body hair either by scrubbing it with pumice stone or using a depilatory cream. Sometimes they even used razors.

At one time, Europeans used this recipe to get rid of unwanted hair.

Hair remover
Florentine iris root 1 oz (28 g) [for perfume]
sulfur ½ oz (14g)
niter [potassium nitrate] ½ oz (14g)
lye made with ashes of bean stalks, 1 quart (1l)
Mix all together and boyle it so long in a glaz'd earthenware pot till putting a pen [feather] therein all the feathers peel off.

You tested the potion with a feather because feathers and hair are both made of keratin. The smell would have been awful, even with the iris root for perfume, but the potassium sulfide produced would have removed hair.

In the 14th and 15th centuries, Spanish and Italian women raised their hairlines with stuff like this, and removed their eyebrows and sometimes their eyelashes, too, to produce a high, bald forehead. So did some of the men. A century or two later, Mexicans were crazy about low foreheads, on men and women.

The Pits
Armpits produce hair and harbor scents, and a lot of effort has gone into removing both of them. Here's a deodorant from 1665, already using a form of aluminum (alum) like modern deodorants:
If you bathe the armpits with any sort of alum dissolv'd in water, it will condense the pores, and hinder the sweat from streeming through the skin.

Today many people like to pretend the only smell they have comes out of a bottle. They deodorize their own smell with chemicals, usually aluminum chlorhydrate, then use perfume in soap, cologne, or aftershave.

The five hairs
Ancient Indians sometimes shaved their belly hair into patterns, but shaved off their chest and pubic hair. Today, some Indian holy men shave off all their "five hairs": head hair, whiskers, chest hair, underarm hair, and pubic hair. Some teachers have their disciples pluck out their head hair and whiskers to avoid shaving.

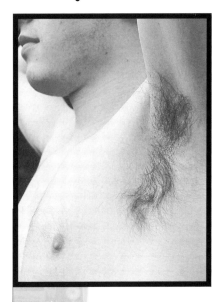

facial HAIR

Whiskers

"It is impossible for a beardless man to enter the Kingdom of Heaven," claimed a group of Russian churchmen in the 16th century. Men used to swear by their beards and were deeply ashamed if forced to shave them off as punishment.

Upper-class men in ancient Egypt shaved their faces and wore stiff false beards for special occasions; the longer the beard, the higher the rank. Hatshepsut, the only woman in ancient Egypt to rule as a pharaoh, wore an artificial beard at ceremonies to show her status.

The Babylonians and Assyrians were keen on false beards, perhaps because they favored such ornate styles. Those in the upper classes had their hair and beards carefully dressed and curled, plaited, and waved. But fashions change. In 1351, a Spanish king thundered: "Let no man dare to wear or to make any false or contrived beard."

Older Arab men were said to dye their beards red, and Persians blackened their beards even before they went gray.

Shaving beards has been outlawed by the Taliban, an Islamic government in Afghanistan. Men without beards had their heads publicly shaved, and government officials were sacked if they had insufficient facial hair. According to the Taliban, Mohammed didn't shave, and neither should anyone else.

At the World Beard and Mustache Championships, whiskers of all shapes, lengths, and styles are paraded and judged. There are 15 different classes of facial hair, as well as "free style," for more inventive types. The longest mustache belongs to a man in Rajasthan in India. It stretches for 11 feet, 11 inches (3.7 m) from end to end.

Beards today

Hippies loved beards, and at one time artists were all supposed to have plenty of facial hair. Recently, beards have been less popular. There is the rugged look, where men keep their whiskers just long enough to look as if they haven't shaved for two days. And some guys are into precision shaving: goatees, tufts of hair under the bottom lip, and so on.

A sad and saintly story of a bearded woman

In a church in Prague there is an effigy of a bearded woman in a blue dress — a saint. She wanted a religious life and refused to marry the man her father had chosen for her. Her prayers to God to save her from the marriage were answered — God caused her to grow a beard, and her fiance rejected her. Outraged, the woman's father killed her, and she became a martyr.

Hairy noses

Nose hair keeps out dust, but sometimes there's so much hair it can look like you've been sniffing blowflies. Tough men and women pluck them; timid ones use special nostril-trimming scissors.

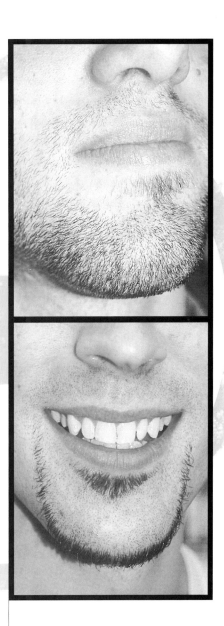

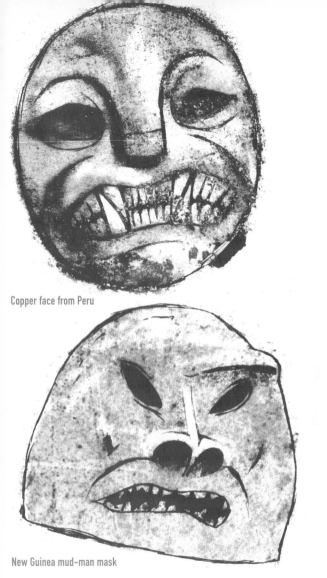

Copper face from Peru

New Guinea mud-man mask

Children love to play dress up, and so do many adults. Bodies can be decorated, shaped, or disguised in masks, hats, headdresses, jewelry, shoes, clothes, codpieces...and there are plenty of fake bits and pieces to stick on, too.

masks

A mask can change or disguise someone, help its wearer tell stories, frighten enemies, and even ward off disease. And what's a carnival without masks? In Venice, Rio, Bahia, Trinidad, Mardi Gras in New Orleans, and Notting Hill Carnival in Britain, masks allow people to step outside their everyday selves. There are masked balls and fancy-dress parties and of course Halloween.

Half-masks of velvet or taffeta were popular in 16th-century France. They were supposed to protect the wearer against the weather, but were also alluring and mysterious. The British and Dutch liked masks, too, but the French king forbade his courtiers to wear them – he probably wanted to see their shifty eyes.

DRESS UP

Masks have always been important in theater, in ancient Greek drama, medieval mystery plays, commedia dell'arte (Pierrot, Columbine, Harlequin), and Japanese Noh theater, which has more than a hundred named types of mask.

Sometimes masks are worn during initiation ceremonies. The initiating guide may be masked to symbolize a larger force or being; sometimes the initiates are masked to symbolize their new status.

Masks have been popular among the tribal people of Africa and South America, where they are an ancient tradition. (See color inserts.) Secret societies like to wear masks, often for anonymity. Ku Klux Klan members cover their whole head, and the Dukduk of Papua New Guinea wore enormous masks to judge and execute wrongdoers. Masks grant another sort of anonymity to millions of Muslim women, sometimes whether they want it or not. In some countries, these masks cover only part of the face; in others, women are completely covered, with only a slit for their eyes.

A 5-foot- (1.5-m)- high Dukduk mask

Bedouin women with burka face masks, Oman

jeweLry

Fingers have been adorned with rings the world over since the earliest times. Sometimes the rings are elaborately linked with chains to hand and wrist jewelry, as in India; sometimes they are plain bands of metal, wood, or even stone; sometimes are encrusted with gems. Rings are popular with women, but men wear them, too, especially powerful men such as the pope, or kings, princes, and noblemen. Finger rings can indicate whether a person is married or not, but toe rings seem to have less significance.

Wrists and ankles are often decorated with bangles, bracelets, and other jewelry, such as watches, wrist straps of cloth or leather, and so on. And necks have sported everything from massive golden collars to slender strings of shells and beads. Jewelry is an essential part of body piercing, too.

NaiLs

Nails share the mysterious "half-dead, half-alive" quality of hair. In some cultures, nails and hair are buried or burned to prevent an enemy using them to cast evil spells. Nails are also a reminder of the claws we share with other animals, so they can look primitive or feral. Some ancient Maya from Central America let their nails grow into foot-long, twisting, useless claws – imagine the disaster of a broken nail there! In Thailand, dancers achieve a similar but more symmetrical effect with long brass "fingernails." In Manchu China,

the ladies of the court wore long nail protectors made of precious metals, enamels, and jewels. On a plainer note, men in some Mediterranean cultures allow one fingernail, often on the little finger, to grow long.

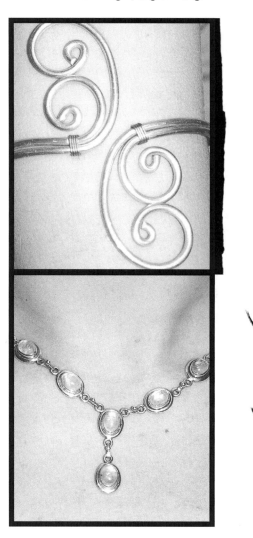

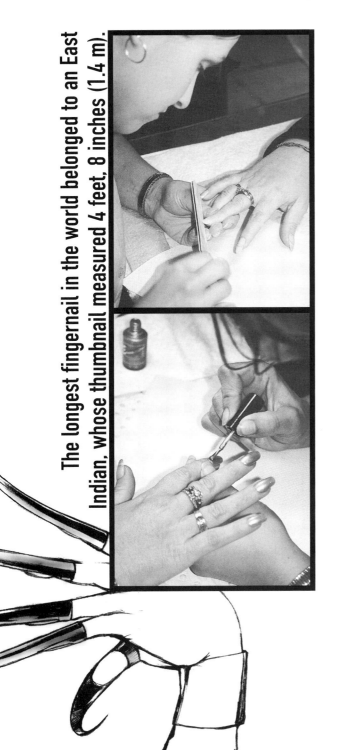

The longest fingernail in the world belonged to an East Indian, whose thumbnail measured 4 feet, 8 inches (1.4 m).

manicures and pedicures

Nails on both hands and feet can be manicured, decorated, and colored. Manicured nails signify leisure, wealth, and the absence of hard manual labor, which plays havoc with nails.

In ancient India people wore their nails long and polished, unless they were nuns; nuns were banned from manicures or any other frivolities.

"I hate nail extensions: they can really damage your nails. I'll do them if someone asks, but I don't like it."

Selby, beauty therapist

Some women fake it with a set of chunky acrylic nails or nail extensions. It's a complicated process, involving sanding, glues, acrylics, and solvents. If the nail grows out, filler is used in the gap, but if a nail snaps off you must start from scratch. A plain old manicure sounds like more fun. The manicurist soaks the nails, pushes back the cuticle with a stone or orange stick, then nips back excessive cuticle growth. After nail buffing, hand cream, and massage you may want nail polish. Today you can choose from a whole host of colors, from blood red through yellow, green, and blue to black, with or without glitter. In some communities, nail decoration has become almost an art form, and nails are decorated with stripes, spots, flowers, and other designs.

SHOES

High-heeled shoes make the leg muscles more shapely and tilt the spine to thrust out the breasts and backside. They also make it hard to walk and almost impossible to run.

At one time, women in the imperial court in China wore beautiful embroidered slippers with thick platform soles that tapered toward the base. They were supposed to give a woman a graceful, willowy walk, but there must have been a few turned ankles.

European men and women in the Middle Ages wore shoes with extra-long points. Church and governments tried unsuccessfully to restrict the length of shoes, but by the time winklepickers became popular in the 1960s, governments had given up trying to censor shoes.

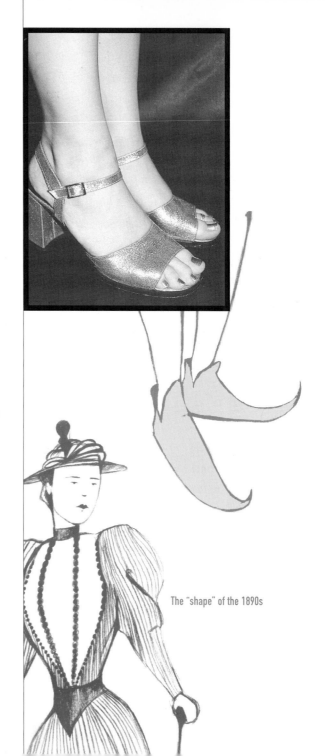

BRA WONDERS

The quickest way for a women to change her breasts is to buy a bra. In the Western world, bras and underwear have shaped breasts to the latest fashion:

- full, smooth, and rounded, like a pigeon's (1890s)
- flat and boyish (1920s)
- big, round, and impressive (1930s–40s)
- sharp, high, and pointy (1950s)
- natural and braless (1960s–70s)

Today there are underwire bras, to thrust the breasts up and create cleavage; padded bras, to make them bigger; sports bras for support; maternity bras for breast-feeding; T-shirt bras for a smooth "natural" look, and so on.

The "shape" of the 1890s

DRESSING the PENIS

A tailor may ask a man which side he "dresses" on, to find out which side of the trousers should have an allowance for the penis. But there are many more ways of dressing a penis than that.

The Namba people in the New Hebrides are named after the pidgin word for "penis wrapper." The Small Nambas wear a penis wrapper of banana leaves, while the Big Nambas at the north end of the island wear a more impressive affair of purple-dyed pandanus leaves.

Yanomami men from the Amazon tie a thread around their foreskins so they can anchor their penises to their belts. Another impressive look is the penis gourd, a long, curving, pointed gourd attached to the penis and anchored with a belt.

Codpieces

The earliest codpieces, or genital coverings, were worn by the Minoans in ancient Crete. They came back into fashion in 16th-century Europe when jackets got shorter and the Church insisted on men covering their genitals properly. The men were only too happy to agree, and covered their bumps with elaborately padded codpieces decorated with jewelry, lace, and bows. These were spacious enough to be used as pockets or wallets, and strong enough to support a flagpole during a procession.

Codpiece from 16th–century Spain

91

fLatHeaDs

Mangbetu mother and baby

Unhappy with the shape of your head? Blame your parents. When you were a baby, your skull was like modeling clay; they could have shaped it, but it's too late to do anything about it now.

Some parents elongate babies' skulls by binding them tightly; others tie on boards to flatten them to a fashionable shape. Such changes have been practiced on almost every continent – for eons.

It can be a class thing, too. Aristocratic Greeks and Romans shaped their babies' skulls, and upper-class Mangbetu babies in central Africa used to have their heads re-formed with two planks bound on tightly with strips of bark. Long head shapes were desirable, and they were supposed to encourage intelligence and protect the children against witchcraft. High hairstyles supported by ivory sticks made the heads look even longer.

The Chinooks of northwestern North America thought a distorted skull was a status symbol,

RESHAPING tHE BODY

too.
And it was easy to identify slaves because their heads weren't pointed or flattened. The ancient Maya of Central America used wooden molds to flatten a baby's forehead and push the brain cavity out at the sides. Only 200 years ago, French country people tied a linen bandeau around the baby's head to shape it.

Cockeyed?
Long ago, the Maya people hung a stone in front of every baby's brow so that it would become slightly cross-eyed, and therefore more attractive.

If you are unhappy about the color of your eyes, you can change it. Colored contact lenses allow even dark-eyed people to try blue eyes, or green, or gray, or even violet.

teetH

"I was just out of year 6. my teeth were very crooked. I had a really bad bite. mom and the orthodontist decided. "

josie, age 24

In many wealthy countries, straight white teeth are the ideal and crooked or buck teeth are increasingly rare. But the cattle-herding Toposa people of Africa love prominent teeth so much that they remove their lower teeth so the upper ones will stick out. Then their teeth resemble those of their beloved cows rather than ugly goat's teeth.

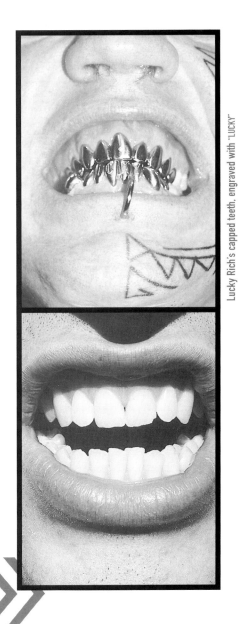

Lucky Rich's capped teeth, engraved with "LUCKY"

DRaCuLa aND CO.

Vampires aren't the only ones who find pointy teeth attractive. In Africa, Dogon myths describe the sharp, pointy teeth of the ancestor spirits who first combed out the threads of speech. These threads were woven on a loom symbolized by the mouth. To reflect these myths, the Dogon people either chip, file, or color their teeth, and the women pierce their lower lips and wear a ring through the center of them. Without it they are naked, and to be naked is to be speechless.

In Sumatra, Mentawei Islanders have their teeth filed to points like a shark's teeth. In Bali, teeth are filed down till they are even. It's a mark of adulthood, and it's supposed to protect a person from the evil side of human nature. Without filed teeth a person cannot be cremated safely, because the gods might mistake them for a fanged demon and throw them out of the spirit world.

The Maya people of Central America traditionally filed their teeth to fine points and inserted decorative infills of stone, gold, or obsidian. Some rock stars have had a diamond inserted in a front tooth for an instant flashing smile, and occasionally people will have an infill shaped like a star, or a colored gem set into a front tooth. Wealthy people still have gold teeth, especially in Europe.

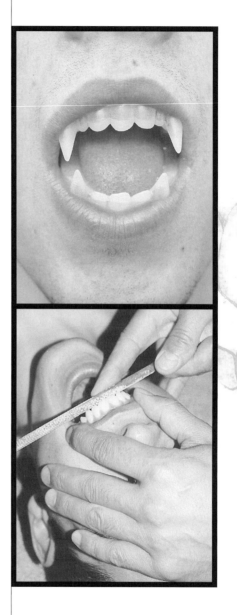

False teeth

The Romans could have false teeth made of ivory, gold, or wood. In fact, the first laws of Rome refer to them.

By the 18th century, false teeth were still uncommon in Europe and America. Made from wood, bone, ivory, rock crystal, enamel, porcelain, or gold, they were often held in place, more or less, with wires. George Washington, the first U.S. President, wore false teeth, which occasionally dropped out in public. His teeth were probably made of ivory.

Knock knock

Some Aboriginal tribes knocked out one or more front teeth when a person was being initiated. In one method, the person bit down on a block of wood, while another person tapped at the front tooth with sticks, using them like a hammer and chisel.

Big Namba women from the New Hebrides have their front teeth knocked out as the mark of a good, hardworking, married woman. And a brave one! During the very painful ceremony the woman does not cry. Afterward a warm plant stem is pressed against the wound to stop the bleeding.

Toothpaste

Want whiter teeth? Try stale urine. That's what some Spaniards and ancient Romans used. It was also supposed to keep the teeth and gums healthy and firm.

In India, twig toothbrushes and tooth powders or pastes were used thousands of years ago. They are still used in many places today. In England, there was powdered pumice stone mixed with vinegar, or sticks made of powdered coral and gum. Both were a bit tough on the enamel.

RUBBER-Necking

Padaung hill tribe women, who live on the border of Thailand and Myanmar, once elongated their necks with metal rings, earning themselves the name "giraffe women." (See color inserts.) Brass-covered rattan rings were added to every girl's neck as she grew, gradually lowering her collar-bones and ribs and elongating her neck. The necks could stretch up to 15 inches (38 cm), displacing vertebrae. An extra-long neck was a status symbol and a sign of a woman's submission to her husband.

There are stories about women having their neck rings removed as a punishment for running off with another man. Their necks were so weak that they had to lie down from that day on. Only older women wear these outlawed rings now.

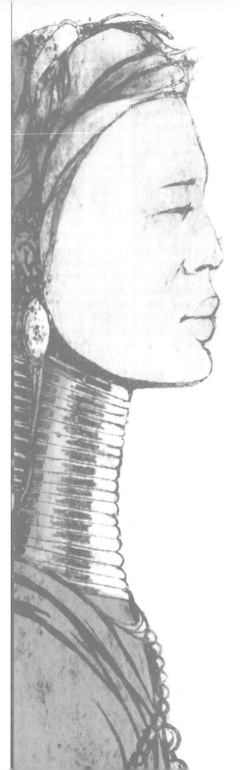

beautiful bodies

Pump it up!

Bodybuilders want to increase the size of their bodies, but only in certain ways and in certain places. They want muscle but not fat. To do this they eat special diets and train with weights to build up their muscle mass and reduce their body fat. Some even take steroids to speed up the process, but these drugs can cause high blood pressure, damage the liver, shrivel the testicles, and make women hairy.

Many movie stars train with weights for particular roles. They pump up their muscles, then allow themselves to return to normal after the film.

People in different places around the world value strong, shapely arms. One way to emphasize the muscles of the upper arm is to bind a tight band below them, just above the biceps. This is popular from the Pacific to Africa to the Americas.

Hands up

Some East Indian holy men choose an unusual way to control their bodies — they hold one arm up in the air for years on end. These *ek-bahu babas*, or one-armed teachers, end up with a wasted arm, fringed with long, curled fingernails. Others choose to have a wasted leg.

Legs

In Liberia, women's legs used to be welded into heavy metal anklets, which they wore for the rest of their lives. Today, thanks to a government ban, they wear none at all, or much lighter ones that can be removed.

Butende girls from Uganda have wide metal bracelets placed on their arms and legs in childhood. As the girl grows to womanhood, the muscles on either side of the bracelets bulge dramatically.

A more flexible form of leg binding has developed on the San Blas Islands in the Caribbean. Cuna Indian women wear brightly colored cords wrapped around their calves and knotted together, as they have probably done for at least 500 years. Christopher Columbus reported that the "Caribs" wore them when he "discovered" America. Then, young Carib girls had 2-inch- (5-cm) wide bands of cloth wound round their ankles and just below their knees, which produced plumply swelling calf muscles, but bound sections that were little more than skin and bone.

Panare men of southern Venezuela wrap their legs in rope made of hair cut from their own and their wives' heads.

Calves

In the 18th century, European men used to strap false calves on their legs under their tight breeches to make their legs more shapely and attractive. Today, some men have silicone implants inserted in their calves by a plastic surgeon.

The leg bindings of Kayaw women from Myanmar reshape their legs

aLL sHaPes aND sIze

In many cultures, people have gone on special fattening diets to look more attractive and prosperous. In West Africa, girls were sent to a fattening house before they were shown to prospective husbands. They were forbidden exercise and fed like prize stock. Women in harems in the Middle East were fattened up for the pleasure of their husbands. Plump women were once popular in Europe, too. The poet Robert Herrick described the ideal 17th-century beauty: *Black and rowling is her eye, Double chinn'd, and forehead high....*

Today in Western countries it's the reverse. The media present images of very tall, very thin models with narrow hips and broad shoulders – in fact, women who look more like young men. Statistically, these women are very unusual, but there's an increasing pressure to fit a slim ideal, for guys, too. So women, and some men, go on special diets to try to lose weight. But crash diets can lead to a cycle of dieting and weight gain.

Some girls and women, and fewer boys and men, suffer from a disease called anorexia nervosa, in which they starve themselves. Nobdy knows what causes anorexia, but images of skeletal fashion models may be a contributing factor.

At the same time, people in wealthy countries are growing more obese, and diets and weight-loss clinics are increasingly popular. Something's not right. Recent studies found that although the Dutch ate amounts similar to the amounts eaten by neighboring Europeans, they had far fewer obese people. Why? Bicycles probably, so plenty of exercise.

corsets — women's wear?

Corsets have been around for thousands of years. In Bronze-Age Crete, corseted young Minoan women and men enjoyed bull vaulting. This dangerous and violently energetic sport required loincloths, codpieces, and tight corsets. These may have been to protect against ruptures while the Minoans leaped over bulls, but they were also decorative. One expert believed that boys and girls were riveted into metal belts between the ages of five and ten and wore them for the rest of their lives. Female acrobats also wore steel-ribbed corsets, possibly for support as well as appearance.

Corsets have been a popular item for the last 300 years. In 17th-century Europe, women wore iron corsets to give a flat, smooth line to their bodices. There were holes cut out for the breasts in some models, but other corsets just flattened them.

A century ago, Russians on the Black Sea wore very tight corsets of bark or leather. In other parts of Europe, baby girls' waists were encased in a tight band that was changed only when she literally split her sides. Women ended up with an hourglass figure – deformed tiny waists, and enlarged hips and chests.

Corsets have worked their way into the English language:
- an uncorseted woman was a "loose" woman (not morally and physically upright)
- a "staid" woman (steadfast and proper) came from the word "stays," or corset
- "strait-laced" women (strict and puritanical) were tightly laced into their corsets

In the 1920s breast flatteners and elastic girdles removed women's curves. Women transformed their "feminine" shapes and their place in society, demanding the vote and equal rights.

In 1945, after the Second World War, women were supposed to leave their wartime jobs to the men and go back home and look wasp-waisted and fragile. They pinched in their waists with a small corset called a "waspie." Then, in the 1960s and 1970s, corsets and bras were thrown out for a more natural look, and women's rights were back on the agenda.

But guys like corsets, too. Tribal men in New Guinea and Africa wear them. In southern Sudan, for ceremonies, Dinka men wear beautiful beaded corsets, reaching down towards the tailbone and up to a point above the shoulders at the back supported by rigid wires. The colors indicate the man's status or age: 15–25, red and black; 26–30, pink and purple; over 30, yellow.

In the 1820s in Europe, some dandies wore corsets, and there was a rumor that American men often wore corsets, too.

Grandmother of pearl

One man currently famous for nothing more than wearing a corset is "Pearl." It took him four years to reduce his waist by half to 17 inches (43 cm). He wears a corset at all times, and can breathe only with the top half of his lungs. He speaks very softly, eats only morsels of food, and can't afford to get anxious in case he suffocates! Pearl claims that he, like many other corset enthusiasts, grew up in a very religious family, where he used to help lace his grandmother into a tight pink satin corset. Tight lacing is about controlling oneself, according to Pearl.

People who are really unhappy with their looks (or perhaps just plain unhappy) reach for the knife. In fact, they pay expensive plastic surgeons to reach for their knives, scalpels, lasers, suction pumps, and silicone. You're far more likely to do it if you're American (or female), and far less likely to do it if you're Scandinavian (or male) – perhaps Scandinavians are more interested in what's under the skin. In the United States, men have only 16 percent of the country's cosmetic facial surgery.

Plastic surgery began as a way of repairing hideously injured soldiers after the First World War. It is still used to repair the effects of burns, injuries, disease, and congenital deformities, and to turn elderly stars into bizarrely smooth-faced mannequins.

face Lifts

A face lift can cost thousands of dollars and take two to five hours, depending on what you have done. Here's what you get for your money in a full face lift:

1. A general anesthetic.
2. A long cut around your face, behind your ear, and under your chin. Don't worry, it's behind your hairline, so your hair hides the scar.
3. Your face skinned – a bit like skinning a chicken. After it's separated from the underlying tissue, it's pulled back out of the way.
4. Fat suction, or liposuction. If you have fat around your chin and neck, it's sucked out.
5. Your face muscles lifted and sewn in place.
6. Your skin replaced. First it's unrolled and lifted, then the excess is trimmed off, and the rest is sewn back along the incision line.

What can go wrong? Facial nerves can be damaged, leaving you with a paralyzed forehead, for example, or even a paralyzed lower lip. Infections and blood clots can also cause trouble.

eye openers

If eyes are the windows of the soul, plastic surgeons are the window dressers. They lift sagging eyelids, remove bags under the eyes, and get rid of wrinkles. An eyelid-lift is similar to a face lift. Fat can be removed by making incisions inside the eyelids, so scars don't show. To remove wrinkles, the skin may be given a superficial laser burn. This causes scarring in certain layers of the skin, which tightens the surface.

Usually the surgery is successful, but sometimes it isn't, and you might be left with:

- Eye of the hare. Hares in legend sleep with their eyes open, and so do some unfortunate people who have their eyelids lifted a bit too high. Eyes that can't close dry out and become ulcerated.
- Round eye. When too much tissue is taken from a bottom eyelid, the eye can't close and too much of the eyeball is exposed. Sometimes the eyelid can turn inside out.
- Pigment changes or blotches.

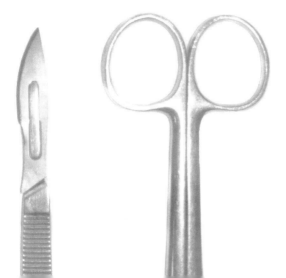

There are also eyebrow-lifts. A plastic surgeon makes small holes in the scalp behind the hairline and draws up the muscles under the forehead and eyebrows, tightening them and sewing them in place.

Deadly beauty

Belladonna means beautiful woman. It's an extract from the deadly nightshade plant that dilates the pupils and makes the eye look larger, darker, and more exciting. But atropine, the active ingredient in *belladonna*, can cause blindness. If it is absorbed through the skin, it causes paralysis, then heart failure. Doctors still use it today — very carefully.

all ears

Jug handles? A taxi with the doors open? Mean jokes about boys with big ears abound. Some people, usually boys and men, have their ears "pinned back" surgically. But plastic surgeons sometimes like to wait until boys "grow into their ears" and their heads and necks reach their full size.

Special ear picks for removing wax have been used for at least 2,000 years in India and other countries. And for those with hairy ears, there were tweezers and razors.

NOSE JOBS

Michael Jackson took things to extremes – he had a plastic surgeon turn his wide nose into a skinny little number with pinched nostrils. Depending on what you dislike about your nose, you can have:

- the tip reduced by removing cartilage
- a low or flat bridge built up with bone, perhaps from a rib; a silicone implant; or cartilage from an ear
- a bump reduced by incisions inside the nose, cartilage shaved off, and then bones broken at the base and pulled closer together
- a wide nose narrowed at the nostrils by wedges of skin and tissue removed from each nostril near the face and the nostrils pulled closer together.

But be warned, your face may look bland afterward, or you may end up with a drooping nose, or have trouble breathing.

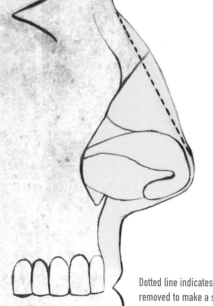

Dotted line indicates the bone and cartilage to be removed to make a straight nose

CHEEKS AND CHIN

In wealthy countries it's possible to have a plastic surgeon insert cheek implants to plump out the cheeks, or to have the shape of your chin altered.

Chins can be made more or less prominent, with bone chipped away or added from a rib. Double chins can be treated with liposuction and tightened up as part of a face lift.

GRIT YOUR teeth

In the West, adults endure dramatic operations to correct their bite. A person with a prominent lower jaw and weak upper jaw can have the lower jaw split and excess bone removed, then the two parts rejoined with titanium. The upper jaw can be moved forward. Sometimes, if there isn't enough bone, part of a rib is grafted into the gap. All that so the top and bottom teeth meet properly.

Dentists also cap teeth, covering the sharpened remains of teeth with white porcelain enamel. Implants are a new but expensive way to get straight white teeth. The dentist screws a nickel titanium foundation into the jawbone to replace the root, and bone grows through small holes in the metal. A white enamel crown is then screwed onto this "fixture."

feet

Generations of women in China had their feet bound to attract men. The custom began among dancers in the Song Dynasty, which ruled in the 10th and 11th centuries.

This is how feet were bound:

Note: This practice is now illegal.

The procedure required long strips of very
firm cloth; water and alum; and one small girl,
sometimes as young as four.

1. The child's feet were bathed in a solution of
alum. Her toes were bent under and pressed hard
toward the center of the foot. The toes were bound
very tightly. Sometimes the big toe was bound
separately to bend it upward. Then, the feet were
forced into tiny shoes.

2. The girl was encouraged to walk a lot so the
bones in her feet would break more easily.

3. In ten days, the bindings were removed and the
feet were washed again in alum. The flesh would
peel and corns would develop, which were cut off
to reduce the amount of flesh. The feet often oozed
blood and pus, but were bound again tightly and
forced into even smaller shoes.

4. This procedure was continued for at least 40
days or up to two years, until the size of the foot
was less than 4 inches (10 cm).

5. The groove between the heel and ball of the foot
would, ideally, be deep enough to contain several
coins; the toes would be curled right under the foot
and the big toe would curl upward to make what
was considered an attractive shape.

Troubleshooting

If the girl tried to loosen the bandages or refused to
walk because of the pain, she was beaten. In hot
weather, her feet swelled and caused extra suffering.
In winter, they were numb from the cold and from
restricted circulation. Sometimes the girl would lose
one or more toes, which rather spoiled the effect.

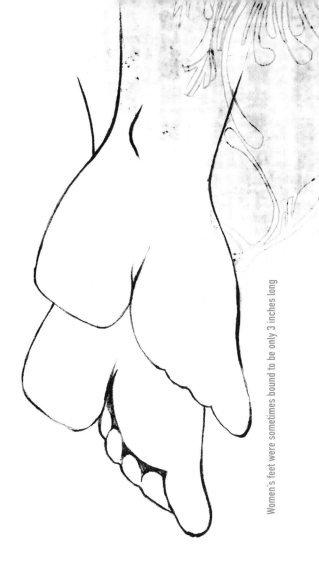

Women's feet were sometimes bound to be only 3 inches long

Once the feet had been reduced to the right size, they had to be bound for the rest of the girl's life to keep them small.

Ordinary working women had their feet bound to a mere 5 inches (12.5 cm), about the size of a toddler's foot. They could still walk almost normally and carry heavy loads, but other ordinary pastimes, like a swim or a stroll in the rain, were impossible. Bound feet caused trouble if they got wet.

The richest women, and prostitutes, had the smallest feet – sometimes bound to as little as 3 inches (7.5 cm). They were then decorated with minute embroidered shoes. It was difficult to walk, and fat or pregnant women had to be helped along.

Foot binding was outlawed in 1911, but for many women it was too late. Their feet could never be normal, and unbinding them was as painful as when their feet were first bound and broken. There are still old women today whose feet are deformed by foot binding.

Walking shoes for regular feet

amputations

Would you amputate your little toe to fit into narrow, pointy shoes? Some people do. According to the *Journal of Podiatry,* toe amputations increase whenever narrow, pointy shoes become fashionable.

Amputate a joint of one finger and replace it with a metal one? That's popular with some goths, especially in San Francisco. (If you're faint hearted, you can wear a metal sheath over one finger.)

A missing fingertip is often the trademark of Japanese *yakuza,* or gangsters – a very permanent show of loyalty to a crime boss and the criminal life.

Aborigines sometimes used to amputate a finger as a sign of mourning; so did certain people in America, Africa, and the Pacific. The Fijians sometimes amputated a toe as a sign of mourning.

In Paleolithic cave paintings in Europe, hand prints sometimes show a missing finger, so the practice may be ancient, or perhaps someone just slipped when sharpening an ax.

bosoms

Breasts have been flattened, squashed, pushed, enlarged, reduced, and cut off. The legendary Amazons were supposed to have removed their right breasts, perhaps to improve their aim with bow and arrow; the Skoptsy (a Russian religious sect given to self-mutilation) removed both nipples for religious reasons; and under Mesopotamian law both breasts could be removed as a punishment. In the 16th and 17th centuries, women's bodices were cut so low that they showed the entire breast. Long before, Minoan women exposed their breasts and wore tight bands at the waist to produce a slender, curvy figure. Beginning in the Old Kingdom and continuing for centuries, Egyptian women wore tunics that left the breasts uncovered, too.

Silicone valley

According to Pamela Anderson Lee, "every single person in Los Angeles" has had breast implants, like she once had. She's exaggerating, but plastic surgery is one of the most common ways of altering the shape of breasts, and even of chests. Men are having silicone bags inserted under their pectoral muscles to make their chests bulge.

The bad news

Not everyone is happy with their breast implants. Even Pamela Anderson Lee has had hers removed. Scar tissue can form around the bags, whether they contain silicone or saline, compacting and hardening them. Massaging the implants and breasts twice a day can stop the scar tissue from sticking to the bag, but it hurts a lot, and it may force chemicals out of the bag and into you. On top of this, the scars where the bags were inserted can also harden. The implants may have to be done several times to get them right. And they only last a certain time – almost all women will live long enough to need a replacement.

Women also have their breasts altered by plastic surgery. These operations, too, are not without problems, such as:

- lopsided breasts
- nipples put back in the wrong place
- "fallout," when breast tissue seems to fall or settle at the bottom and sides of the breast
- large scars
- nipples that do not work properly.

Abreast of fashion

Big or small depends on your culture. The French have always preferred "pretty, small, and firm" breasts. Today, more French women have breast reductions than enlargements, and the ideal breast size (measured around the body and over the breasts) is about 33 inches (85 cm). In America the ideal is about 39 inches (1 m), and in Australia, somewhere in between.

One French physician published a recipe in 1530 for a breast cream containing herbal extracts, turpentine, chicken fat, and calves' foot jelly. After rubbing it on for two or three months, it was supposed to reduce, improve, and firm up the breasts.

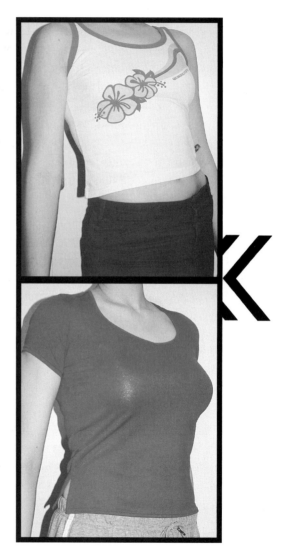

safety first

Whatever you choose to do to your body, make sure it's safe. Anything that pierces the skin – tattooists' needles, piercing needles and instruments, scalpels – must be sterile. Otherwise bacteria or viruses – including HIV, any of the hepatitis varieties, and many others – could be introduced into your body. **They could be deadly**.

Remember, piercing can do permanent damage to nerves and underlying tissue. You could lose sensation, or suffer paralysis of certain muscles, or , if you're a female, make breast-feeding difficult or impossible. Other surgical procedures carry different risks. Make sure you are well informed before you agree to them. Some people have died or been permanently incapacitated or suffered chronic illness because they have tried to change their appearance.

Anyone working on your body needs to know about sterile procedures. If the operator does not wear gloves, leave. If the premises look dirty, leave. If the operator cannot assure you that all equipment is sterile, leave. An instrument is not necessarily sterile if it is:

• held in a candle flame or any other heat source

• dipped in alcohol

• boiled or frozen

Sterilizing instruments should be done by a professional, using an autoclave or another recognized method.

Before you decide on an operator, check the health and safety requirements for your state for piercing, tattooing, plastic surgery, or whatever. You may want to ask:

• if operators need to be registered, qualified, or experienced

• what safety precautions are necessary for your procedure

• if there is an age limit for certain procedures

• if there is a professional body with certain standards for members

• if there are any health risks attached to certain procedures.

It's a good idea to shop around before you decide on a procedure, a place, or an operator, especially if you are planning to change your body permanently. Gather as much information as you can and go to a place that has a good reputation and a good record. Once you have had the treatment, follow any instructions for wound care carefully. Seek help at once if the wound becomes infected or inflamed.

Breaking the skin isn't the only risky procedure. Make sure you know what you are putting *on* your skin or your hair. Is it safe? Will it cause an allergic response? Will it affect any medication you are taking? And will it give you the desired result?

Remember, it's your body — beautiful or bizarre, it's up to you.

bibliography

Asser, Joyce. *Historic Hairdressing*. London: Pitman, 1966.

Badt, Karin Luisa. *Hair There and Everywhere*. Chicago: Chicago Children's Press, 1994.

Bianchi, Robert S. "Tattoo in Ancient Egypt," in Arnold Rubin, ed. *Marks of Civilisation: Artistic Transformations of the Human Body*. Los Angeles: University of California Press, 1988.

Brain, Robert. *Art and Society in Africa*. London: Longman, 1980.

__. *Rites Black and White*. Ringwood: Penguin Books, 1979.

__. *The Decorated Body*. London: Hutchinson, 1979.

__. *The Last Primitive Peoples*. New York: Crown Publishers, 1976.

Breast Implant Information Booklet. Canberra: Commonwealth Department of Health and Family Services, Publications Production Unit, 1998.

Cole, Keith. *The Aborigines of Arnhem Land*. Adelaide: Rigby, 1979.

Cox, J. *An Illustrated Dictionary of Hairdressing and Wig Making*. London: Batsford, 1984.

Dalby, Liza, C. D. *Kimono: Fashioning Culture*. New Haven: Yale University Press, 1993.

Ebin, Victoria. *The Body Decorated*. New York: Thames and Hudson, 1979.

Encyclopaedia Britannica, 15th ed. Chicago: Encyclopaedia Britannica, 1994.

Faris, James C. *Nuba Personal Art*. London: Duckworth, 1972.

__. "Significance of Differences in the Male and Female Personal Art of the Southeast Nuba," in Arnold Rubin, ed. *Marks of Civilisation: Artistic Transformations of the Human Body*. Los Angeles: University of California Press, 1988.

Finkelstein, Joanne. *The Fashioned Self*. Philadelphia: Temple University Press, 1991.

Fisher, Angela. *Africa Adorned*. New York: Abrams, 1984.

Fussell, S. W. *Muscle: Confessions of an Unlikely Bodybuilder*. New York: Poseidon Press, 1991.

Gupta, S. P. *Costumes, Textiles, Cosmetics and Coiffures in Ancient and Medieval India*. Delhi: Oriental Publishers for the Indian Archaeological Society, 1973.

Harkness, Libby. *Skin Deep: A Consumer's Guide to Cosmetic Surgery in Australia*. Sydney: Doubleday, 1994.

Horn, Marilyn J. *The Second Skin: An Interdisciplinary Study of Clothing*. Boston: Houghton Mifflin, 1975.

Horton, David, ed. *Encyclopaedia of Aboriginal Australia*. Canberra: Aboriginal Studies Press for the Australian Institute of Aboriginal and Torres Strait Islanders, 1994.

Jacobs, Julian. *The Nagas: Hill People of Northeast India*. New York: Thames and Hudson, 1990.

Jaguer, Jeff. *The Tattoo: A Pictorial History*. Horndean Hants, England: Milestone, 1990.

Keyes, Jean. *A History of Women's Hairstyles 1500-1965*. London: Methuen, 1967.

Kirk, Malcolm. *Man As Art*. London: Thames and Hudson, 1981.

Kunzl, David. *Fashion and Fetishism: A Social History of the Corset, Tight-lacing and Other Forms of Body Sculpture in the West*. Totowa, N.J.: Rowman and Littlefield, 1982.

Leuzinger, Elsy. *The Art of Black Africa*. New York: Rizzoli, 1977.

Levy, Howard S. *Chinese Footbinding: The History of the Curious Erotic Custom*. London: Spearman, 1970.

McLaughlin, Terence. *The Gilded Lily*. London: Cassell, 1972.

Polhemus, Ted. *Body Styles*. Luton Beds, England: Lennard Publishing and Channel 4 Television Co., 1988.

__. *Social Aspects of the Human Body: A Reader of Key Texts*. Harmondsworth, England: Penguin, 1978.

__. *Street Style from Sidewalk to Catwalk*. New York: Thames and Hudson, 1996.

Powell, Gillian. *Body Decoration* . Hove, East Sussex, England: Wayland, 1994.

Prior, Natalie Jane. *Bog Bodies*. St. Leonards, England: Allen and Unwin, 1994.

Randall, Housk, and Ted Polhemus. *The Customised Body*. London: Serpents Tail, 1996.

Ricciardi, Mirella. *Vanishing Africa*. London: Collins, 1974.

__. *Vanishing Amazon*. New York: Abrams, 1991.

Riefenstahl, Leni. *The People of Kau*. London: Colling, 1976.

Sagay, Esi. *African Hairstyles*. London: Heinemann Educational Books, 1983.

Steele, Valerie. *Fetish, Fashion, Sex and Power*. New York: Oxford University Press, 1996.

Strathern, Andrew and Marilyn. *Self Decoration in Mt. Hagen*. London: G. Duckworth, 1971.

Synnott, Anthony. *The Body Social: Symbolism, Self and Society*. London: Routledge, 1993.

Taylor, Lou. *Mourning Dress: A Costume and Social History*. London: Allen and Unwin, 1983.

The Age, December 1, 1996.

Thèvoz, Michel. *The Painted Body*. New York: Skira/Rizzoli, 1984.

Trasko, Mary. *Daring Do's: A History of Extraordinary Hair*. Paris: Flammarion, 1994.

Tweedie, Penny. *This My Country: A View of Arnhem Land*. Sydney: Collins 1985.

Who magazine, November 4, 1996.

Winter, Ruth. *A Consumer Dictionary of Cosmetic Ingredients*. New York: Crown Publishers, 1974.

Wojcik, Daniel. *Punk and Neo-Tribal Body Art*. Mississippi: University Press of Mississippi, 1995.

www.sfmuseum.org/hist1/subjects.htm; http://ericir.syr.edu/projects [footbinding; Museum of San Francisco]

INDEX

Boldface indicates illustrations.

PHOTO CREDITS

David Altheim: Australian girl (front cover, right); tattooed man, sports fan (color inserts); and all the contemporary black & white photographs other than those listed below. David Altheim's photos on pages: 9, 10, 89 courtesy of Your Body Beautiful; 37, courtesy of Fox Body Piercing Studio; 46, courtesy of Alien Tattoos; 47, courtesy of Smart Arts Tattoo Studio; and 52, courtesy of Nikk Crow, OneTribe Body Pierce Studio.

A.N.T. Photo Library: Solomon Islands mud-men ©Ron & Valerie Taylor/A.N.T. Photo Library; PNG wigman ©Frithfoto/A.N.T. Photo Library; Aboriginal boy ©Klaus Uhlenhut/A.N.T. Photo Library (color inserts); Warrior from Irian Jaya ©Ron & Valerie Taylor/A.N.T. Photo Library (p. 54).
Coo-ee Picture Library: African girl (p. 67).

Coo-ee Historical Picture Library: Maori chief (p. 39, top); Zulu warrior (p. 71).

Matt Darby Photography: Hindu sadhu (p. 36).

Victor Englebert Photography: Fulani man (frontcover, left); Fulani women (back cover); Fulani nomad, Yanomami Indian, Somba *griot,* Turkana nomad elder, Dayak girl, Devil mask (color inserts); Fulani nomad (p. 34); Cuna Indian girl (p. 54); Turkana nomad (p. 68); Tuareg nomad (p. 73); Girl from Cotonou (p. 79).
Great Southern Stock: Nepali woman (p. 17); Oman women ©Graham Simmons (p. 87).

Mayu Kanamori: Head of tattoo club (p 42), preserved tattooed skin (p. 42).

Lonely Planet Images: Buddhist monks ©Bernard Napthine (color inserts); Kathakali dancer ©Eddie Gerald (color inserts and p. 22); Thai woman ©Mark Kirby (color inserts); boy as Hindu god ©Greg Elms (color inserts).

The Photo Library-Sydney: Berber woman ©Tony Stone (color inserts); Samburu warrior ©Tony Stone (color inserts); Surma woman © C. Beckwith & A. Fisher (color inserts); Geisha ©The Photo Library-Sydney (color inserts); Sumo wrestlers ©Hand Heus (p. 71).
Lucky Rich: portraits (p. 45, p. 93, top).
Emmanuel Santos: Jewish men (color inserts); Aboriginal dancers (p. 30).

Underworld Gym: weights (p. 97); cycles (p. 99).

Ruth Lathlean, World Images: hairdresser's board, Nigeria (p. 79).